Non, Je Ne Regrette Rien

NON, JE NE REGRETTE RIEN

Peter Green

The Book Guild Ltd.
Sussex, England

The Book Guild Ltd.
25 High Street,
Lewes, Sussex

First published 1993

Set in Baskerville
Typesetting by Raven Typesetters
Ellesmere Port, South Wirral
Printed in Great Britain by
Antony Rowe Ltd.
Chippenham, Wiltshire.

A catalogue record for this book
is available from the British Library

ISBN 0 86332 833 4

CONTENTS

LIST OF CENTRE SECTION ILLUSTRATIONS

TO SHEENA FOR TOTALLY DISRUPTING HER LIFE

Sheena is a red setter. Although a pedigree, she is small and lacks those wispy feathers that gives the breed its aristocratic elegance. Indeed all the dog experts had chosen her brothers and sisters in preference to her, she being the last to leave her mother's side. Even so she was our beloved and loving pet.

Going to France for a year caused endless discussion as to what to do with her. Should we bring her with us and then have to leave her in quarantine for six months on our return? Should we leave her in kennels? Should we try to persuade a friend to take on the responsibility?

Having her with us in France was very tempting. She would have a field to run in. There would be cows to cower from and rabbits to chase. The thought of her being cooped up in some quarantine cage for six months, put us off the idea though. We had great faith in the local kennels, yet the cost would have been enormous. On the other hand it would be unfair to burden a friend with some of her madder idiosyncrasies, like barking persistently when the telephone rang, and at the same time chasing round in a tight circle, as if angry with her tail. We decided to mention our difficulty in front of friends, hoping for a positive reaction.

Most responses were a concerned, 'What a shame!' or 'You do have a problem.'

There never seemed to be that important glint of dog-loving sympathy. Even when I described how cold and uncaring being in quarantine might be, I failed to breach their emotional armour. One friend, after a few barrier-breaking pints, did offer his services if we were really stuck. When he mentioned the suggestion to his wife he received a stare which was a mixture of disapproval and anger. I did not pursue the matter.

I resorted to telephoning more distant friends. I tried Mary.

'My house is too small. My cat will never get on with a dog. OK, I'll give it a try.'

Mary is a woman of impulse. Before the second impulse could reverse her decision, I quickly accepted her offer and arranged to bring Sheena for a trial period.

After a few days I tentatively phoned her.

'Did you know she loves cat food? Sooty and Sheena hate each other. I didn't see Sooty for two days. She's lovely! I'll do it!'

'But what about your cat?'

'That's OK now. Sooty lives upstairs, Sheena rules down.'

Mary loves a challenge . . . I think.

During our first two months in France I never telephoned Mary. I reasoned that if there were a problem, Mary would phone us. Deep down I knew that frequent contact would ruffle my conscience too much.

During our autumn break in England, we decided to give Mary a surprise visit. She was out. Sheena's prowess as a guard dog must have been the gossip of the neighbourhood, for the backdoor was unlocked. In defiance of possible criminal proceedings we entered. We expected Sheena to rush up to us as usual with tail wagging lethally. Instead she sleepily roused herself from her cushion and almost sheepishly padded over to us. We overpowered her with affection, but instead of pawing for more, she retired to her cushion, seemingly unimpressed by our efforts. It was then I noticed a dark slit down her middle. We left a case of wine and a note, and departed, knowing we would phone at the earliest possible moment.

That evening I found that Sheena had only just returned from the vets, having had an operation to cure the dog's equivalent of peritonitis. I felt terrible. When trying to persuade Mary to look after our dog, I had purposely glossed over the fact that Sheena had only just recovered from one of a number of urinal problems. Rather than the lively companion I had promised, she had become a limp invalid. Mary was adamant that she would continue looking after her. It was obvious that during her illness Mary had become very attached to Sheena. This was particularly apparent during subsequent phone calls.

Mary would make comments like, 'I'll really miss her when you have her back.'

It was evident that a new problem had arisen. Should we take back Sheena? Or should we upset our children and leave her in her new comfortable home?

1

BRIGHT IDEAS AND SCEPTICAL FACES

'Right then, let's drop everything and live in France for a year.' I can still hear the echo of the words that I flung across the dining table at my wife, Polly. Do not be deceived, though! It was not my authoritative boldness which had instigated these remarks.

Polly and I, two hours earlier, had sat down with a Chinese takeaway and a bottle of red wine, 'très ordinaire'. The meal had begun with some general thoughts about our working day. Polly then started to talk about the need for change and for her to grasp any opportunity to speak French on a regular basis again. I nodded and mumbled my agreement. Then I uttered a remark which I am still reminded of whenever I am in a more negative frame of mind.

'Wouldn't it be nice to have a few months in France?'

It was almost a condescending throw-away comment, but it was snapped up by Polly who developed a multitude of reasons as to why it was such a good idea.

'What an experience for the children! They'd be half way to being bilingual! Think of the benefits to your French! It could also lead to our careers going in completely different directions!'

I jovially agreed. It was a marvellous dream, but the possibility of such a radical move was out of the question.

'Think of the weather! Remember what it was like when we. . . ? There'd be wine on tap! What about the Beaujolais when we. . . ? And those cheap French restaurants! That meal in. . . !

The memories glowed.

The conversation started to change tack. A seriousness as well as enthusiasm was now in Polly's voice.

'We'll sell the house. And then we've got cash in the bank. We'll be able to afford it. Let the children have a full year in a French school. They'll speak fluently.'

My reactions to these thoughts were defensive.

'If we come out of the house market completely, it could be a big mistake. A whole year without either of us earning a sou! We'd be mad! What about the kids' friends? They'd be so upset leaving them. They'd hate every minute out there.'

We continued in this vein for some time, with Polly's comments becoming more and more plausible and persuasive. The idea was both exciting and appealing, yet I had to express a more sober point of view. After all, part of my conditioned upbringing was to appreciate having a settled job and an undisturbed way of life.

'We've got to keep our feet on the ground. Jobs won't grow on trees when we come back.'

This voice of common sense was sounding like a series of hackneyed sayings. It was no good. I was agreeing with too many of Polly's remarks.

She was in the middle of stressing how refreshing a year without work would be, when I interrupted her abruptly with: 'Right, let's drop everything and live in France for a year.'

The silence that tells that something important has happened lasted for three or four seconds. Then it was another bottle of wine and a further two hours of planning and preparation.

The telling time came in the morning, when ideas developed through night-time exuberance can appear limp and uninviting.

'Do you still want to do it?'

'Let's go for it!'

The ball had been set in motion, and we were both stubborn enough not to back out without a very good reason.

* * *

When we first decided to live in France, I was curious to know what our friends and associates would think about our decision. For the most part our acquaintances showed enthusiasm. What I did notice, though, was a certain scepticism. This was most apparent when we said we would not be working in

France. A more mumbled, stuttery response was then evident. I was prepared to push aside a stable future to follow an uncharted path, with no economic gain.

At the same time I detected a chink of envy in their reactions. That impression of, 'If only . . . .' may have been given by a whispered sigh, a thoughtful gaze into the distance or, as in one or two cases, the divulging of pipe dreams. One wanted to live on the inland waterways and run a barge hotel. Another, who included the odd French phrase (in a distinctive Yorkshire accent) in her everyday, English conversation, has always wanted to live in France and learn the language properly.

Everyone has a dream. It may be of possessing sporting prowess, being with a pop idol or having a dynamically interesting job. For the most part it remains a fantasy, and little real effort to turn the dream into reality is made. Perhaps most people need the unattainable as a safety valve against rash behaviour. Anyway, is it not so, that reaching your goal leads to dissatisfaction? Ask the character Dudley Moore played in *Ten* or a big pools winner, five years later.

This type of thinking must have been in the back of the mind of a work colleague who, with refreshing honesty, declined the more obvious pleasantries. He wished us luck but said we were brave and a little foolish. He didn't say why we were foolhardy, but the loss of job stability seemed the most likely reason.

There is much to be said for his philosophy. The chances of Polly and I gaining the jobs we wanted in the area we wanted, as soon as we came back from France, were remote. We knew we would almost certainly have to accept a drop in salary. In spite of this, I had the innate belief that we could gain employment and maintain a reasonable standard of living on our return. Our newly found language skills could in fact enhance our prospects. Surely it was not too drastic to try something a little out of the ordinary, to have a mid-life period of jobless relaxation.

A malaise of our times may be that we have already gone so far along the road of civilization as to take the bite from our existence. Could not one of the root causes of our numerous social diseases be that we are rejecting enterprise and challenge? Our comfortable standard of living is suppressing something that is basic, human instinct.

The people who were our long-standing friends reacted

differently. There was a passion in their response and wholehearted support for the idea. It was most reassuring to know that those closest to us could see the overall benefits such an experience could bring. There is much to be said for kindred spirits.

We had decided to live in Brittany, despite the warmth of southern France being an attractive proposition. We felt that easy access to Britain was preferable to a perpetual suntan. Being able to visit friends and relatives with minimal disruption was going to be particularly important to the children.

Whether to rent or buy caused us little consternation. If the collateral from the house were well-invested, it would give us an income. Had we bought, the amount of interest made would be negligible. We also might have to sell a purchased property quickly, in order to reestablish ourselves in Britain at the end of our stay. There were definitely too many difficulties in buying.

Polly kindly volunteered to have a long weekend in Brittany, to look at some of the rented accommodation available. She managed to survive the driving eccentricities of various French estate agents and returned to recommend the most expensive house she had seen. She had obviously fallen in love with it. Despite my hard swallow at the thought of the extra cost, it had to be the right place. Not only was it a beautiful house but it had that precious commodity of space both inside and out. Being able to have friends staying with us was a big reason for the appeal of the idea originally. In this house we could cater for many people. It was exactly what we wanted.

The only bureaucratic problem we had in wanting to live abroad lay in our attempt to acquire long-stay visas. I first asked for the appropriate forms to be sent to us in May, four months before our proposed departure. After an ambition-killing wait, they arrived in early July. I was horrified to find they had to be completed in French. Because of her greater proficiency in the language, visas suddenly became Polly's domain. This was not appreciated, particularly as each form had to be written out six times. A photocopied version was evidently thought to be open to greater criminal manipulation. The possibility of illegal emigration was also behind the Visa Office's invitation for Polly and I to go to London, with all relevant documents on an appointed day at the end of July.

When we arrived inside the visa building we were confronted

by the tail end of a queue. On peering through a glass divide, we realized that the queue snaked its way along a corridor and into a large, packed waiting-room. There must have been anything up to 120 people in front of us.

We dutifully waited in the queue, shuffling forward a few inches every now and then. This movement was caused, though, by hopeful expectation and the belief that closing the gap on the person in front would lead to being dealt with more quickly. In fact only seven people had left in twenty minutes. Thoughts of being asked to come back tomorrow, when only a few metres from a hatch and having to sleep on the pavement, in order to be first the next day, flickered through my mind.

I started talking to the man in front of us, whose wildly coloured shirt seemed better suited to a Caribbean island than our sombre corridor. He informed me that most people were not trying to leave the country but to stay in it. Further investigation was necessary. We pushed our way into the waiting-room, avoiding the harsh stares from the static queue, and found that the only unattended hatch was the one we wanted.

Our forms were checked and found to be in order. We happily waited for our visas to be passed through the hatch. None were forthcoming. I asked for them but was told that this was just the beginning of the process. Two and a half months was the beginning of the process? We were reassured that we could still go to France, but we would have to come back to London to collect our visas. The thought of the cost of four people having to return to Britain, in order to be handed two visas personally, was a little galling. I would have been only too pleased to pay for them to be sent by registered letter.

Our disappointment at not getting our visas was tempered by the sight of the drained faces of those in the still massive queue. My friend with the flamboyant shirt was in the corridor, no more than a few metres further on than before. He had hours to wait for his precious six-week extension to his stay in Britain.

We had been in France five months when we next had communication about our visas. More information was required. We decided to ignore the letter and rely on the fact that we would be abroad for no longer than three months at a time, if any questions were asked. So we became 'illegal immigrants', albeit of the short stay variety. We heard nothing further.

* * *

On the day of our departure we and our possessions were staying with Keith and Annita in Bristol. It would take two and a half hours at the most to catch the 12.30 ferry from Portsmouth. Leaving at 9.30 would get us there in good time. Brian, Polly's brother, had volunteered to help transport our luggage. To fit everything into two cars was going to be difficult, but Brian and I were confident we could do it.

On the day of departure everybody was up early. We did not, though, possess the weary-eyed look which heralded a working day. We were bright, sharp and busy. The cases, bags and boxes were soon piled up outside. We cajoled, shoved and squeezed as much as we could into the cars, but there was still a mass of belongings strewn on the pavement. Radical thinking was necessary. At the bottom of Brian's car was a cardboard wardrobe, in which lay our most precious items of clothing, flat and uncreased. It meant completely unloading his car, but the wardrobe had to go.

After twenty minutes the car was repacked with many of these garments screwed up to fill any visible crack. A few boxes and sundry items were not catered for, but these had been purposely left until last as they were less essential. Any thought of using the rear view mirror had long since disappeared.

We set off at 9.45. Rather than go by convoy, we arranged to meet at a certain service station half-way to Portsmouth. It took until the first road junction before we had to stop. A box and bag had deposited themselves on to Kate's head and lap. Either she and Luke had to keep these things in place with their heads and extended arms for the rest of the journey, or another arrangement was required. Further manipulation of our possessions was accomplished but not in the more subtle and creative way, as was the case when first loading the cars. Instead we crammed and wedged items, unconcerned about the possibility of ripping the roof lining with our less than tolerant approach.

We arrived at the service station without any further traumas, only to find, to our surprise, that Brian was not yet there. He was going to use the longer motorway route, but his more powerful car should have enabled him to reach the service area in good time. We waited half an hour, but there was no sign of him. We surmised that he had arrived much earlier and decided to go on alone. In Portsmouth he was neither waiting outside the ferry port nor on board. It was looking to be a disastrous first day for our extravaganza.

2

LATE, LOUD AND FLUSTERED

Several reasons for Brian not making the ferry were mooted while we were on board: he had broken down, he had waited for us at a different service area, the heaviness of our luggage had caused the suspension to come adrift from the rest of the car. It is strange that in such situations the least wanted possibility is the one mentioned last or not at all. This was the case here, for the thought that Brian had been in an accident was never put into words.

Brian would be bound to telephone Keith and Annita in Bristol! Polly phoned them but Keith had heard nothing. He did volunteer, though, to rearrange his social programme and stay in, in case Brian did call. It was good to note that we had left behind some genuine friends in Britain – Keith and, so it appeared, Brian.

Our last hope was that Brian had boarded the *Sea Cat*, which was due to reach Cherbourg about three hours after we did. We went for a walk, had a meal, watched some struggling crabs being hauled in from a trawler and took up position near where the cars were due to drive off the boat. Our task was made easier by the fact that only nine cars had been on the *Sea Cat* (its teething problems had been well reported in the British press), and sure enough one of them was Brian's.

Explanations were soon forthcoming. He had been held up by roadworks and assumed that we would be similarly delayed. Therefore he had waited at the appointed service station, despite knowing he would miss the ferry. He did not have our address, so once in France he was going to find a *pension* for the night. He was then expecting to spend the next day on an extended sightseeing tour of the backroads surrounding

Moncontour, looking for a blue Volkswagen with English number-plates.

Our previous tensions having disappeared, we relaxed and joked for a quarter of an hour, before departing (in convoy this time) for our destination. Polly drove ahead of Brian while I navigated. This may not have been the best plan, as I found it hard to decipher the relevant road signs quickly enough. It is always difficult to adjust to a new country's set of road signs. By the time I had spotted and worked out what a sign meant, there was a fair chance we would have passed the turning we needed. Taking a wrong turning on a beautiful, hot, summer day can be very rewarding, as it can introduce you to delightful territory, unmolested by the tourist. At night-time, though, when you want to get to your new home as soon as possible, it can be just a trifle disconcerting.

Another problem, that slowed us down from time to time, was caused by Brian's headlights. Before setting off from Bristol, I had dutifully given my headlights a very generous coating of yellow paint, to comply with the continental regulations. (The bright, yellow lights of French cars are much easier to cope with than the glaring, white headlights to be found in Britain.) Brian, on the other hand, had given his headlights a very thin coating of paint. As a result many French drivers, not appreciating the piercing quality of his lights, felt honour-bound to express their feelings on the matter by giving us full beam.

An additional error of judgement was made by going the most direct route according to the map. Instead of travelling along main roads, adding about nine or ten kilometres to our journey, we decided to go as the crow flies. Had a crow used a road map to ascertain his route, he would certainly have gone that way. Having travelled along it for a kilometre or two, he would surely have rejected both road and map. It weaved its way through the countryside, unconcerned for Roman road ideology. At times its structure was erratic, something that was exaggerated by our overladen vehicles. It certainly made me realize the reason for one of the French expressions for a hump in the road, *un dos d'âne*, meaning back of a donkey.

Just before midnight we easily found the turning leading to our house off the Moncontour road. There was also no problem in finding the sign with our house's name, *La Ville Méen*, on it.

This is where our difficulties began. We were to discover later that La Ville Méen was the name for the conglomeration of houses in the vicinity. So there were a number of signs indicating the name of the house, but none of them were helpful enough to say it was the Ville Méen which had been recently purchased by some British people. Polly had seen the house many months previously, but her memory of its whereabouts was uncertain and her sense of direction was disorientated by the dark.

We first drove into one of the farmhouses in the area. We soon realized our error but were prevented from making a stealthy retreat by two Alsatians who bounded towards the cars. They started barking with a raucous violence which deterred any thoughts of knocking on the farm door to enquire where our house was. They had no fear of being run over, for even as we were in the process of retreating, they were performing their teeth-baring duties no more than a foot away from our car windows. We tried a nearby house but were greeted by another dog, smaller and less fearsome, yet just as noisy. Polly and Brian's reversing started to lose its normal, calm authority as the frustration of the situation increased. We shot off in the other direction down a dusty lane. Our journey was short-lived, as Polly screeched to a halt to prevent hitting a wire stretched across the track.

It was time for a rethink! Justin, one of the joint owners of the house, had stayed in France to meet and greet us. He had said he would leave the lights on in the house if we arrived late. It was simple! We had to look for a house with light beaming through its windows. Our plan was foiled by the fact that every house was lit up as a result of the noise we had created. Having caused this midnight disturbance, we were disinclined to knock and ask anyone. We decided to try some of the smaller tracks. So it was back past the farmhouse again. This time the dogs were waiting for us on the edges of their residence. Their greeting, though, was less vociferous than before.

We found a narrow track down which the bushes occasionally brushed the sides of the cars. At the bottom was a sharp, left-hand turn. Again we came to an immediate halt. We were now faced, not by wire, but tall, ripening corn. There was no room to turn, so reversing was the only choice. This proved no easy matter, as the rear view mirror was totally ineffective, and on either side of the track were two overgrown ditches, ready to envelop any stray car wheels. This called for much use of clutch and accelerator. (I am sure the neighbours would have testified to this fact.) In addition I had got out and was attempting to help the drivers by means of vigorous, sometimes incomprehensible, arm movements. After two close shaves Brian and Polly had managed to extract themselves from the cornfield and its treacherous ditches, and were ready for further exhilarating adventures.

There were two more abortive attempts before we spotted a fairly narrow track to the side of one of the houses we had passed previously. Rather than repeat our earlier experience, I volunteered to explore on foot. Within half a dozen steps I heard the near hysterical yapping of a dog behind me. With the eyes of my children upon me, not to mention two adults with the potential for excessively cutting sarcasm, I decided not to run. Instead I walked quickly, trying subtly to increase my speed as the dog's high-pitched barks came nearer. In only a few seconds it was jumping up at my back. My hands shot to the level of my head, in true Western-style submission. I had felt losing clothing preferable to flesh. I also turned my head to see what venomous beast was attacking me. In so doing I half-stumbled, at the same time kicking the dog as it was about to jump up at me again. The dog was a tiny thing of cosmopolitan pedigree, whose main aim was merely to say, 'hello'. Despite its obvious, harmless nature, I declined to give it a pat, heeding my own warning to the children not to touch stray dogs. Even so, it carried on jumping by my side as I continued down the track, until the end of its territory or its boredom plateau was reached.

At the bottom of the drive I thankfully came upon our house. Frantic arm-waving and thumbs-up signs persuaded Polly and Brian to drive down the track and on to the gravel, parking area. Justin came out to meet us. The cars were unloaded, the bedding was sorted and the children flopped into bed. We then relaxed with a glass of beer, while we recounted our fraught day to Justin. Sleeping proved no problem that first night.

The morning brought the chance to take a good look at the house. It had been an eighteenth century barn, which had been converted about fifteen years previously. The children loved the place. Their bedrooms were large with beautiful, wooden floors and the more modern shutters, which can be opened and closed from inside. In between was a huge room that we decided would be their playroom, (unless the house was brimming with guests). The whole of the upstairs was their territory and they tackled the task of unpacking their toys and books, with the zest of a first-time housebuyer. Their other joy was the field adjoining the house. They had never had such a large, outdoor, playing area before. It was soon to become an inspiration for their imagination.

Polly and I loved our new home just as much as our children did. The lounge-cum-dining room was magnificent with thick, stone walls, an open fire and wooden beams. These beams had a character all their own. They lacked the more clinical lines of a recent era. They were gnarled and twisted their way from one wall to the other, rejecting any symmetrical niceties. It seemed possible to imagine the shapes of the original trees they were cut from. Attached to two of the beams were two thick, wooden hooks. We never found out the actual reason for them being there, yet their presence used to fire our visitors' imaginations.

Our bedroom was next to the lounge and was again striking because of the stonework. There was also a spare bedroom, known as the dungeon, on ground floor level, which was almost an after-thought on the end of the house. Its nickname was given because it had a very small door, forcing adults into unnatural positions in order to enter. There was also no direct access to the rest of the house. This meant that visitors had to brave the open air, before coming through the front door, to go to the toilet. Some, it was rumoured, never even made the front door. If a number of guests were staying, Polly and I would consider their respective nocturnal habits (if indeed we knew them), before suggesting who should sleep upstairs and who in the dungeon.

The dungeon in fact was a very pleasant room, despite its drawbacks. It gave guests a certain privacy which would certainly be missing had they stayed in the rest of the house. Indeed nearly every visitor who was offered the choice elected to sleep in the dungeon in preference to the possibility of a bright-eyed energetic child greeting them at six o'clock in the morning.

On ground floor level there was tiling throughout, the type which would not allow glasses and china to bounce and remain intact. In Britain fitted carpets and softer kitchen flooring often gave such items a second chance. At first we were breaking things every other day, though after a while, mindful of extravagances, breakages became far less frequent.

The furniture in the house was not ostentatious, though there were one or two very attractive pieces. What it did have, though, was a distinctly French feel to it. Indeed the whole house did.

Justin's presence was a bonus. He had remained in France to make sure everything was tidy and in good working order, and to help us by passing on the names of his contacts and knowledge of the surrounding area. Polly's sixth sense was right; the warmth the owners possessed was somehow embodied in the house itself.

On the Sunday Justin was very willing to help in any way he could but was also keen to give me some information about the house and some of its idiosyncrasies. He introduced me to the workings of the central heating system in the boiler room, attached to the side of the house. Like the dungeon, its only entrance was from outside.

I soon realized that, in order to turn on the heating, someone had to go outside into the boiler room and flick a switch. Doing this at seven o'clock in the morning in February to warm the house up for everyone did not excite me. Justin explained that the central heating didn't really warm the house on its own. More thoughts of February! There was one aspect of the heating system that he hadn't managed to work out, though an explanation was in the information leaflet. The oiliness of this leaflet indicated that he had tried very hard to sort it out, suggesting that my own efforts would lead to a similar outcome. Instruction leaflets have always been an anomaly to me, so I expected little success with ones written in French.

We moved back inside and sat in the lounge. Justin then started to tell me about the various wild life of note. He had not seen a viper around the house but he had assured me that there were many more in Brittany than Britain, and it was probably best to keep looking down on a regular basis, when walking around the field. My normal, proud, upright gait would definitely have to be adjusted. Then he mentioned, looking at me for any sign of flinching, that the spiders were large, very large.

Mice were next. Their presence was the one thing that people, who had used the house as a holiday home, had complained about. I laughed confidently, suggesting that this would be but a trifle to us. He added that he had detected an unpleasant smell near the sideboard. Though he hadn't found the root cause, he suspected mice. I sniffed in the vicinity and inwardly agreed with his assumptions, assuring him that this was no problem.

Further conversation followed, about our past and hopes for the future. Then a strong, rustling sound came from a carrier bag full of food, brought with us from Britain, which was resting in the far corner of the lounge. The rustling turned to crunching. Justin investigated and over his hand jumped a small, harvest mouse who scurried swiftly under the sideboard. This led to the decision that the shopping should be unpacked. As a result we discovered that the Ryvita packet had not only been entered, but that six Ryvita biscuits had exceedingly frayed edges. We were less concerned about the mouse's excellent choice of dietary food than the possibility that this sweet-looking creature had infested the whole packet. In the bin it went!

About a quarter of an hour after Justin's departure for St Malo on his 'sit-up-and-beg' bike (he had got the French bug for cycling), while relaxing over a coffee, our Ryvita mouse reappeared, looking for its second course. With considerably less forthrightness than Justin had shown, I stretched out a leg tentatively in the direction of the mouse and tapped my toe on the ground. No reaction! A stamp with the same foot succeeded in disturbing it and our friend disappeared again under the sideboard.

'Perhaps French field mice, as well as foxes, have rabies,' I told myself, trying to give myself a logical reason for my cowardice.

There is a great deal of truth told in the children's story of the town mouse and the country mouse. The country mouse has a bold naivety which the town mouse would never contemplate. The town mouse would surely laugh at our Ryvita mouse's openness and lack of real concern or fear of the human enemy. It is sad to think that if we were picnicking in a field, and a harvest mouse was bending an ear of corn, oblivious of our presence a few feet away, we would watch, feeling unchallenged, with child-like awe. Yet as soon as that same mouse crosses the threshold of our house, it possesses evil attributes. It carries and leaves disease with every footstep. Its movements are menacing and it induces an illogical fear, which cannot be alleviated until the beast has been killed.

The rest of the day was spent unpacking, exploring Moncontour, as close to a French-style evening meal as we could manage and a wine-affected chat about the previous day's activity. The latter took place over a log fire, a necessity not because of the cold, but because of the need for the right atmosphere.

The next morning we said our goodbyes and thanks to Brian and set about cleaning the house from top to bottom. It is strange that, even if a house you move into has been exquisitely scrubbed and polished prior to your arrival, you still need to make your own mark on your new place by going over the whole process again. This activity led to the discovery of the source of the unpleasant smell. Justin had been right, for lying with the pawns of the chess set, was a dead mouse. The status of its companions became more significant as the year unfolded.

3

THEY EVEN KISS THE DINNER LADIES

We had purposely arrived in France only a day before nine-year-old Kate and seven-year-old Luke were due to start at Moncontour School. We felt it would minimize their concern. It certainly appeared to, as the excitement of the new house seemed to outweigh fear of the unknown.

Everyone was up early the next day. Polly and I were lively, confident and enthusiastic. Kate and Luke were quiet and thoughtful.

I imagined them thinking, 'They're not normally so bright and cheerful. What on earth are they trying to hide?'

One thing we were trying to hide was guilt at dragging them out to France (for their own good, of course), and propelling them without any real assistance into the French education system.

We all went to school that Monday. As we waited to meet the head teacher, Madame Ecobichon, Kate and Luke were both tense and silent, bemused by the incoherent jabber to be heard in the play area outside. After form-filling, Madame Ecobichon took the four of us into the playground. Kate and Luke stood by our sides, like petrified animals, shocked into immobility, with only their eyes moving to take in this new world they had been asked to enter. Madame Ecobichon appreciated their difficulty and beckoned a small girl to come and meet them. She was the one English-speaking child in the school. This helped the children (and us) to relax, and we made as unobtrusive a getaway as possible.

Polly and I were apprehensive when we went to pick them up at half past four. This uncertainty increased as neither had come out of the school at the expected finishing time. We were soon to find that the dust of French teachers' cars was not to be seen at the scheduled time of departure. The teachers would quite often arrive after the official starting time, yet could occasionally be found still teaching at ten to five.

Kate was non-committal as to how the day had gone.

Luke said, 'Brilliant!' Then he followed this with, 'They even kiss the dinner ladies!'

Luke had spent the last year and a half hiding behind corners in order to avoid an amicable kiss. To see so many people indulging in this hated activity was amazing to him. We found later that the word 'brilliant' had not specifically referred to the school day, but that Madame Ecobichon had given him a fountain pen, a pencil case and felt tip pens. (We discovered at the end of the month that the word 'given' was not applicable, as we received a bill for them through the post.)

Having to use a fountain pen was a new experience for both Kate and Luke. In many ways it helped improve their handwriting, though Luke had obviously inherited his father's ability to 'spread the word' on to skin, clothing, indeed anything that would thirstily soak up ink.

On arrival at school on Tuesday, there were four children waiting to greet Kate and Luke and involve them in some playground activity. This was not something pre-ordained by the teachers but a natural response to newcomers. The family is a strong unit in France, and this family feeling is transferred into the school situation. There is a togetherness, which is most noticeable when the older children are dealing with the younger ones. They seem mature and responsible, putting up with infants' silly ways and 'mothering' them when necessary.

The children reacted very differently to their new school environment. In the first two or three weeks Kate found it difficult. She had been keen to learn the language, and when faced with total lack of comprehension, felt she was up against an unclimbable stone wall. This also meant that she was unable to develop any real friendships. In Britain she had an uncanny gift for making friends and she was sorely missing them. To develop any close relationship must have seemed an impossibility. There were difficult nights and early mornings. Eventually, though, a deep-rooted tenaciousness began to show through, and she gradually started to cope with her problems.

Luke, on the other hand, outwardly had a far more

nonchalant approach to the situation. He knew we were coming to France for just a year, and I think had decided not to bother learning French. Instead I feel he was inwardly determined to use a rare ability he possesses, that of being content with his own company. After all it was only a year!

In the first few weeks his first line of conversation to anyone he encountered in the playground was, 'Do you speak Eeenglish?' in a mock French accent.

When we tried to help them with their French at home, Luke would decline, stating that he only spoke 'Eeenglish'. This laid-back bravado disappeared after a month, when the true impact of the situation had broken through the frail outer shell he had created for himself. The 'funny tummy' became quite a common occurrence.

This was often brought on by thinking of one of the puddings he had to eat for school dinners. It was prune flan, a Brittany speciality. He had been made to eat it by one of the dinner ladies and it had all but made him physically sick. I understood how he felt, having had a similar experience with baked apple when at school. My sympathy had little effect for he dreaded each lunch hour. At morning break he would specifically look in the dining room, to see whether there were any table spoons set out on the tables. If there were, he knew there was a good chance that there would be *flan* that day.

He was also frightened of the dinner ladies who were loud and forceful. One of the English books I had bought Kate and Luke to read while in France was called *The Scourge of the Dinner Ladies*. On its front cover it had an enormous, food-splattered dinner lady wielding a saucepan with vicious intent. I thought it would help him laugh at the school dinner situation. That picture was evidently too close to reality. He declined to read the book.

When not at school, he would prefer to stay within the security of our house than go out for the day. Sometimes we had to force him into the car to enjoy himself.

The cry-wolf syndrome did rebound on us on one occasion. He had complained of stomach-ache when he had heard that we intended going to Le Val André to have a picnic on the beach.

'We're not staying at home because you decided you don't want us to go out.'

'You never want to do anything.'

'Are you going to stay at home all your life?'

This verbal slating lowered his resistance and persuaded him to get into the car. Throughout the journey Luke said nothing, only managing to produce a watery smile when spoken to.

Earlier that week Kate had perceptively described it as, 'That pretend smile, when he doesn't want to go to school.'

We set out a delightful-looking picnic, but Luke declined to eat anything. More verbal chastisement fell upon him. He despondently ate a little salad and half a yoghurt. Then as we were going for a walk, he deposited breakfast, lunch and probably the previous night's evening meal on the beach. It was our turn to feel bad now. Our impatience and anger had masked the fact that he was genuinely ill. Luckily, being sick gave him a new lease of life and he enjoyed the rest of the day. I didn't though.

Soon Luke's approach to the language began to change, and with it that early morning dislike of school started to disappear. He began to use some of the words he understood and would enquire the meaning of others. He had come to realize the need to use French and was opening his mind to the learning process.

This, along with befriending his minder, led to him being far more content within the school environment. His minder was a warm-hearted, confident girl called Manuella. She had sat next to Luke from the very first day. She looked after him, tried to explain things to him and at times would feel it necessary to remind the teacher that Luke could not do certain tasks. He valued her help and stayed with her at every opportunity. Manuella liked his clowning playfulness. After five or six weeks, a genuine friendship had developed.

Homework proved to be an additional burden. The fact that Kate and Luke had never been given homework in a British school was but a small part of the problem. If adults were to do an intensive course in a language they had not previously encountered for seven and a half hours a day, it would be mentally tiring. To transfer that difficulty to young children who have a much shorter concentration span and then add two or three hours' homework, gives an idea of the extra pressure such work can produce.

I am sure French children would have been able to do the homework in under an hour, and indeed Luke's homework often took less than half an hour, but Kate was involved for much longer. They both homed in on Polly to explain what was required. Her input was essential. She would set aside at least an hour to assist and encourage.

Their homework would include learning poems, phonetics and grammar. Neither had tackled any formal grammar before, so for Kate to understand such concepts as the past historic tense and reflexive pronouns was extremely difficult. She would often go to bed looking mentally drained. The saying used to describe the lot of Parisian workers, '*Métro, boulot, dodo*' (Métro, job, sleep), could to a degree describe Kate on a school day. The exception to her day being totally committed to learning the language and school work was about an hour's play before bed.

I have suggested that homework caused a problem. In reality it was a problem for Polly and me rather than the children. They begrudgingly accepted the situation. Kate in particular was adamant that she did everything she was asked, not wanting to use the excuse that she did not understand to get out of doing the work. I was worried about what effects the extra work would have on them.

'It's hard enough learning a new language, surely they don't need this homework?'

'What good is this doing when they can't even understand the instructions?'

'Doesn't Kate look pale and drawn?'

We discussed the matter regularly. Luckily our uncertainties did not rub off on the children and homework became an accepted part of the school day.

It was in the playground that our children's confidence began to grow, rather than in the classroom. Here they had the unfettered opportunity to communicate, at first through body language. Luke used his arms and legs boldly to draw attention and explain his thoughts. To the French children he was a character, eccentric and likeable. Kate was far more subdued, using a nod, shake of the head or shrug of the shoulders. She communicated very effectively, though, through her involvement in playground games. She is well co-ordinated and took to the games very quickly. This helped to make her respected and liked. She was taking the difficult yet positive steps towards making the type of friendships she desperately missed.

It was also in the playground that their first complex use of language occurred. This was through the medium of the French rhyming song which is an integral part of some of the playground games. Although at first they knew little of what they had sung, it was that all important spontaneous use of language. The favour was returned and many of the French children learned some of the British rhymes and games.

The week before their first half-term break, I felt much more convinced that they had settled in their new school. 'As well as could be expected' best described my thoughts. Such mellow tones could not be used to portray the first week back at school after our half-term holiday spent in England. I felt that a taste of the old life would make Kate and Luke a little depressed for one or two days, when back in France. What I had not legislated for, though, was the turmoil caused by the changes made in Moncontour School.

Madame Ecobichon had left. When choosing the house we were to live in, Polly had talked with Madame Ecobichon. She was impressed by her concern for the individual and although recognizing the centralized requirements of the French education system, seemed prepared to manoeuvre the rules a little, to incorporate some of her own educational principles. We had not been disappointed, for she had been constantly aware of Kate's difficulties and much of the time would give her individual work. The most important thing, though, was that Kate really liked her.

In her stead was Mademoiselle Gerard, a young teacher half-way through her training, who naturally wanted to make an impact on her new class. This she did most vociferously. She regularly used her piercing voice to establish discipline. Her outbursts reverberated around the school.

Even Luke was heard to say, in open-eyed seriousness, 'I can hear her in my classroom. She goes mad!'

Kate was now expected to cover the same work as the others in the class. She simply could not understand most of what she was asked to do. It was little comfort to know that the whole class had been disturbed and that a number of parents had officially complained. Kate was miserable.

Emilie, who was to become Kate's best friend, had also been

upset by the change of teacher. Kate recalled a lesson when Emilie became a little fidgety. Her eyes had that look of intense hatred, which young adolescents have honed to perfection. Her thick glasses helped exaggerate this look.

'Everyone prepare for dictation.'

Almost before Mademoiselle Gerard had finished speaking, Emilie said, 'Kate didn't have to do dictation with Madame Ecobichon.'

Her response was not put in a constructive way, it was aggressive and vindictive. It was as if she had been waiting all lesson for this moment to inflict this psychological wound on her new teacher. Chastisement was immediate and verbally brutal. This, though, was not important to Emilie. Her victory had already been gained.

Luke had a new teacher too, Monsieur Girardot. He was also asked to go to a different class in the mornings, to become involved in some of the more basic language concepts. For Luke the loss of his 'right-hand woman' in the morning was immense. Manuella had been his voice in times of uncertainty. His morning teacher could speak no English and he was lost. He became worried and unhappy.

I was downcast. The feelings of guilt at disrupting our children's cosy world in Britain were surfacing again. We seriously contemplated giving up the idea of living in France. As so often happens with dilemmas of this sort, the decision was to wait and see. Doing nothing had its reward. After a fortnight of extreme discontent, things began to improve.

Luke learned to deal with his divided timetable and became his relaxed normal self. He found that a hangdog expression would touch a particular dinner lady's heart and he would not have to eat his flan. He even read *The Scourge of the Dinner Ladies*.

Mademoiselle Gerard became less tense and her qualities of conscientiousness and concern were more apparent. Kate was no longer overawed by her and was given more consideration because of her language difficulties. She even said she was glad she was doing the same work as the other children, because she didn't feel so separate from them as she had at first. They were both coping again.

Perhaps the most pertinent comment to be made during those two difficult weeks came when Polly said to Kate, 'You may thank us for this year in France one day.'

'One day,' was her tight-lipped reply.

* * *

Within a week of Kate and Luke starting at the school in Moncontour, a parents' meeting was called on a Saturday morning. Polly had only found out when she dropped off the children at the start of the school day. She rushed home to collect me, so I did not miss this opportunity of being involved with such a school activity. Slightly dishevelled and without any breakfast I joined Polly in the car. We hurried back to Moncontour, eager that we should not miss too much vital information.

We need not have worried, for on our arrival there was but one small group of parents in a huddle of serious conversation. The numbers soon increased, and other small groups were formed, similarly intent on discussion. We had been there half an hour when, at about ten o'clock, I think, the meeting actually began. I used the word 'think' because there appeared very little difference between the conversations that took place before ten and what occurred afterwards. It took me some time to work out that in fact someone was in charge of the meeting.

The meeting had been called to protest about the school having its staffing cut from four to three. The school needed eighty pupils to warrant four teachers but it could only muster seventy-six. Clusters of intense parents would fervently discuss a point, then throw it to the assembled throng for consideration. This led to a considerable amount of crossfire and repetition. After about an hour of such activity the closest thing to a decision was that a letter of complaint should be written to the authorities. Even this was a suggestion mentioned four or five times, rather than an official agreement recognized by the meeting. There seemed little hope of any effective protest. This indecision and a stomach, hankering after some breakfast, had started to make me feel fidgety.

My hunger pangs were soon forgotten, though, with the appearance of an unusual-looking man in the doorway. He wore an old tweed jacket, which was at least one size too big for him. His sloping shoulders accentuated its appearance of being a hurried jumble-sale acquisition. His shirt and trousers were creased. His head was bowed, not in humility, but merely so that he could see what was happening over his glasses.

'Obviously it's the caretaker. That is it! The end of the meeting! Nothing achieved! Never mind, the thought was there. Time for brunch.'

The old man's first move was to saunter over to those people nearest the door and shake their hand. He then proceeded to go round the room, greeting everyone in this way.

'This caretaker is subtle, no cry of "everybody out". He is going to make everyone feel uncomfortable so that the meeting will end prematurely.'

This seemed to be working most successfully as the various conversations were noticeably starting to wilt. Then he grabbed a chair and placed it next to the woman in charge of the meeting. He was to be part of the proceedings.

'What are you going to do?'

He inclined his head towards the chairperson, indicating who the question was addressed to, but at the same time, he surveyed his audience over his glasses.

'We will write to the Education Department.'

'And if that does not work?'

Our chairperson shrugged her shoulders. One or two others suggested some further ideas, though they lacked conviction.

'This is what you must do!' he said vehemently, leaning forward, defying anyone to relax their attention for even a second.

He then put forward his plan of attack. And attack it was! The parents had to occupy the school. The press had to be called in. A meeting with the authorities had to be sought. Mutterings of such action being too severe were heard, though I was certain they were far more muted than if someone else had proposed such an approach. Each plea for leniency was dismissed by our new leader: every school in the area had a better teacher/pupil ratio; the Education Department would only act as a result of adverse publicity; there were two new English children in the school who needed additional help! All opposition was silenced with impudent ease.

'Well that's decided then!' he concluded, getting to his feet as he spoke, to stress the finality of his statement.

Amid silence he slowly left the room, leaving the chairperson to implement his decision.

While this was being done, I could see him through the window, surrounded by children clinging to his hands and coat. He was the modern-day equivalent of the Pied Piper. Either that or the other end of the rural community's intellectual spiral – not the village idiot, rather the eccentric village genius.

When the meeting closed, I asked, in true Lone Ranger fashion, 'Who was that man?'

I was surprised to find that he was both the doctor and mayor of Moncontour.

The mayor was the main topic of conversation that evening, as we enjoyed our Brittany-style Coquilles St Jacques. We also talked about the effect of our children being at the school. During the morning's discussion, the additional problems their presence would cause the teachers had been mentioned from time to time. No animosity was evident from these remarks.

I wondered, though, whether this would remain when the extra teacher was refused. After all, whoever heard of a bunch of thirty parents twisting an education committee's arm into giving a school an additional member of staff?

The following Saturday was the day for our first sit-in. The press arrived, the Education Department was contacted and an agreement was reached to meet representatives on the Monday. Further action was to be withheld until after that meeting. The first stage had been successful, apart from the fact that the children had had a protracted two hour playtime at the start of the school day.

On Monday came the astonishing news that the school was to have an extra teacher. Whatever the reasons, the campaign had been successful.

Perhaps it had been the mayor's comparison of the farmers with the parents. Two weeks earlier a protesting group of farmers had slaughtered a lorry load of English lambs. I don't think the educational administrators believed we would kill a child a day to prove our point, but the thought of aggressive protests could have swayed their judgement. This could also have been aided by the photograph of our sit-in in the local newspaper. It focused on two dark, swarthy individuals, whose countenances looked less than friendly. We were evidently a group of savage activists. Perhaps the powers that be did not want attention drawn to some of the deficiencies of the education system. Perhaps the change of heart was for educational reasons!

Such an occurrence is virtually unheard of in Britain. In France it appears to happen quite often and at many different levels. For instance the *lycéens* (the sixteen to eighteen year olds in French schools), managed to extract 4.5 million francs from the government through concerted and at times intimidatory protests. Mr Mitterand, no less, was reported as saying that if they have a voice they must be heard.

4

A RELATIVE BEGINNER

Polly was fairly fluent in French seventeen years ago, when she spent a year just outside Paris. At the start of our escapade she admitted that her French had become rusty. Our two children were at the other end of the spectrum, as they had studied no French and had heard virtually none when living in Britain. (French children have a definite advantage here, as they regularly listen to American and British pop music.) My knowledge of French was somewhere between the two. I had gained a magnificent 'O' level pass twenty-nine years previously. I achieved this by industriously studying two or three text books by the renowned Mr Whitmarsh. This enabled me to conjugate the subjunctive and past historic of the verbs 'to be' and 'to have' effortlessly. Unfortunately it did not tell me what to say if someone asked me how I was.

I soon realized my inadequacies when first encountering France as a student, and immediately decided not to display my inability by speaking in awkward and inaccurate monosyllables. Instead I chose to be British, by pointing and using sign language. This was not always necessary as the French whom I met had a fairly good understanding of English. Therefore, on arrival in France, my knowledge of spoken French was atrocious.

I had already decided that it was imperative that I did not sit back and let Polly do the talking. I had to force myself to communicate at every opportunity. This began in a restaurant soon after our arrival by ferry.

I eagerly pushed through the door first, to be greeted by, '*Bonsoir monsieur.*'

'*Bonsoir madame.*'

Her response was a sentence which included the word *quatre*.

'Four,' I thought, 'she's asking whether I wanted a table for four.'

'*Oui!*' I answered with confidence.

She then said, 'Would you like to sit upstairs or downstairs?' in broken yet very accurate English.

Yes, she had detected my country of origin from hearing a mere three words. Surely this cannot be. My French teacher had told me I had a good accent. Had I in fact been taught by means of the Ted Heath school of thought without realizing it?

I was disappointed but not destroyed. I knew the learning process would be difficult and that I would have many setbacks.

My next encounter with the language was on the following day, after inspecting the oil tank at the back of the house with Justin. To do this we had to step over an electric fence and cross into the field of the neighbouring farmer, Monsieur Gilbert. He was there with his quiet, friendly Alsatians, who had introduced the other side of their nature to us the previous night.

Justin and Monsieur Gilbert talked for a number of minutes, with me understanding very little. Luckily Justin intermittently gave me a synopsis of the conversation. Apparently there had been a spate of thieves stealing oil from people's tanks. Keen to be part of the discussion, I forwarded the single word, 'Iraq', spoken in as good a French accent as I could muster. I had been successful in communicating, as the next five minutes were spent in discussing the Gulf crisis. Again I had virtually no understanding of what was said. On returning to the house, I quite impressed Brian when I said that I had initiated and taken part in a discussion on the Middle East. Polly knew better, though, and prised the truth out of me.

During the first couple of weeks my attempts to speak French seemed always to be in Polly's presence. These invariably were collections of individual words (rarely phrases) that were dragged from my memory. As to do this took time, particularly when trying to concoct a sentence, I had to turn away from the person to whom I was talking. This was done to avoid embarrassment and to help me concentrate. Unfortunately it was also a subconscious cry for help. As a result my eyes often rested on Polly. This usually led to her interrupting my faltering efforts and taking over the conversation. This was the last thing I wanted, for I knew improvement would not come unless I was constantly practising the language.

An animate discussion over a ratatouille and a bottle of wine helped us realize that I needed to speak French without Polly being present. Like an amateur actor who freezes on the first night, I found the presence of a potentially critical audience distracting and inhibiting. Therefore I would volunteer for every little errand that needed doing. I seized at every opportunity to buy milk, *baguettes, pains au chocolat* and particularly *pâtisseries*. I eagerly wanted to deal with bank transactions, pay bills at the town hall and buy stamps at the post office. Around lunchtime my ear was attuned to the sound of the post office van skidding to a halt on the gravel outside the house. I would hurry to the door to receive the mail in person, in order to pass a few basic pleasantries with the postman. Many mistakes were made which went uncorrected, yet I was involved in the speaking of French in as natural a situation as possible, without assistance as soon as a difficulty arose.

This sometimes meant two trips to deal with one situation, as was the case when I attempted to hand in a medical insurance form. An official from St Brieuc came to the *mairie* every Thursday afternoon to deal with medical matters.

I went to see her at an appointed time, expecting to say, 'Hello, here's the form,' and 'Goodbye!'

Instead there were questions, many questions, the last of which was to enquire what work I was doing.

'*Pas de travail*,' came my staccato reply.

There followed the pause, which was almost pre-requisite, whenever we mentioned we weren't working while in France. She then said more fervently that I needed another form, because if we weren't working, it was counted as being on holiday.

A phone call was now required to see which form I should fill in. The call gave us the information that there had been torrential rain in St Brieuc but proved unhelpful in determining which form I needed.

Until now the official, realizing my difficulties with the language, had spoken slowly and repeated herself on many occasions. Such an approach was now forgotten as I received a barrage of French. I understood very little, but guessed that she was forwarding the merits and demerits of forms E 106, 109 and 111.

My contribution to this discussion was, '*Oui*,' whenever she paused for breath.

She obviously thought that this meant that I understood. In fact it meant that I knew very little of what she was saying, but was too polite and embarrassed to ask her to repeat it. What I had wanted to tell her was that we were waiting for our visas which, when they came, would establish the fact that we weren't on holiday. I couldn't find the words to do that. So I left with the vague impression that forms E 109 and 111 had to be obtained, probably from England, before seeing her again in a fortnight. Polly's intervention was needed, and in two weeks' time it took her a mere three minutes to rectify the matter.

I found at first, that if I could plan what I said in advance, I could communicate. Much would depend, though, on the response I received. If it was what I expected the person to say, the conversation could continue. If it was not, a look of panic-stricken blankness would envelop my face. The expression, 'being lost for words', took on a whole new dimension.

Rather than reside passively for a year, hoping that the language would trickle through to me, I felt I had to take positive measures to learn French. I decided to learn five words or phrases a day. These were not to be picked out of the dictionary with a pin, but would come from my various contacts with the language. I would listen to radio and watch television on a regular basis, read French newspapers and magazines and do some kind of voluntary work.

I was fairly self-disciplined in learning these five words a day, though I'll have to admit to having a day of rest on Sundays. The words were listed in my diary and I methodically tested myself each week. Even so there is a definite difference between learning words parrot-fashion and being able to recall them immediately they are needed in conversation.

I particularly remember the time, about half-way through our year, when I wanted to use the word for a standard. I had tested myself on this word for five or six weeks, never getting it wrong. In an actual situation though, the word had disappeared from my mind. I could visualize the page it was written on. I could see some other expressions of paramount importance, such as 'an unlit road', 'to batter to death' and 'it's a dog's life'. But *un niveau* – a standard or level refused to come to me. Retention for a vocabulary test was obviously insufficient to produce a word in that split second required to make spontaneous conversation. It was necessary to listen to it being used on numerous occasions, to see it in context in books and newspapers, as well as trying to use it myself whenever possible. Only then would the word be a natural part of my French vocabulary.

I used television a great deal to listen to the language. At first I watched a wide variety of programmes, mostly from curiosity. In the evenings, films and variety shows seemed most prominent. In the daytime, soaps and quiz shows were popular (the French equivalent of 'The Price Is Right' is on five times a week). I resolved to watch two programmes regularly. One was a half hour mixture of local and national news. The other was a dubbed American soap called *Amour, Gloire et Beauté*.

Even at first I had some understanding of the content of the news programme, despite it being concerned with some complex issues. Many of the longer French words often used on it were the same or similar in English. This enabled me, together with the various, filmed news reports, to have a fair comprehension of what was happening. My confidence was boosted no end.

Amour, Gloire et Beauté was about the fashion world. All the women were immensely attractive, elegant and stunningly dressed. The men were exceedingly handsome (two even had dimpled chins) and their suits, shirts and probably their pants were tailor-made. The acting for the most part was good, yet the production was weak, unless the producer had the likes of me in mind, when creating each half-hour episode. He certainly gave me many clues, if I had not understood what had gone before. For in the middle of a scene a character, unbeknown to all around, would divulge his or her inner thoughts, by means of a statuesque display of feelings.

Picture this example! Brooke (a beautifully proportioned, beautiful woman) is telling something to her brother, Storm (a beautifully proportioned, beautiful man). All I can detect from listening is that it is to do with their father. But then Storm turns to the fireplace. There is a three second take of him staring at the fire, his eyes narrow and glowering and his lips tightly zipped. My mind has time to consider his pose. It is obvious he hates his father. The next three second take is of Brooke, a tear gently nestling on her cheek. (Do they use eye drops or on audition are actresses asked to show their ability to cry at the click of a finger?) Despite her watery eyes, she confidently stares straight at the back of Storm's head. Her head is held high, her chin juts forward. She must have something of emotional significance to tell him. The words are uttered. One of them I recognize – *vivant*. Storm turns round and stares at his sister. His eyes are wide open now, not just with amazement but with that same evil glare; his bottom lip has also been unzipped. For fully five seconds we see Storm like this. It gives me time to assess the situation – father – living – Storm in a state of secondary shock. That is it! Brooke has told him that she has found her father to be alive. Storm storms out.

Through the producer's lack of subtlety, I was able to gain a fairly good idea of what was happening. This was good for my morale, so I watched on a regular basis. As a result, despite never having been drawn to soaps in Britain, I was hooked. I would try and watch every episode. If I missed one, I had to read the synopsis of what happened in the television magazine. And shamefully, just before going back to England, I surreptitiously read five days' worth of synopsis in the magazine section of the supermarket – without paying for the privilege.

French radio aroused no such obsession. I did try and listen, but the language spoken went too quickly for me. It was like playing chess without knowing how each piece moved. There simply weren't enough clues to ascertain the meaning and certainly no time to work out what was being said. So the BBC programmes infiltrated into our lives and became our main connecting link with what was happening in Britain.

I had a regular diet of French newspapers. For the first week I studiously scoured a local newspaper. This soon became tedious and I resorted to flicking through for relevant information. This was partly because there was seldom anything on Moncontour and the surrounding area, but mostly because much of the content was extremely parochial. There might be a meeting in a village to discuss the coming *fête*. The paper would state where and when the meeting took place and that there was a good deal of enthusiasm. Alongside these two sentences would be a picture of fifteen or so stunned and awkward looking people. This type of dynamic news coverage would be repeated perhaps twenty-five times in one paper. The reason behind this, surely, was to get as many people's pictures as possible in the paper, in order to boost sales.

Unfortunately it did not make riveting reading and eventually the national newspapers took their place. These had more meat to them and demanded more concentrated consideration. The extra time and mental energy involved was worthwhile. The combination of seeing French expressions in print and hearing them, led to me using them. The media proved to be of great assistance in improving my language skills.

These aids to language were all to be peripheral. My involvement with voluntary work, perhaps two days a week, was to be the basis for perfecting my French. Before leaving for France I had been led to believe that it would be more difficult to find voluntary work there than in Britain. Therefore, having already shaken hands with the enigmatic mayor of Moncontour, I felt I knew him well enough for him to be my guiding light in this matter.

To the *mairie* I went.

'The mayor is out. Call back this afternoon.'

And in the afternoon – 'He won't be back again today. Try tomorrow at eleven.'

The next day just before eleven – 'You've missed him by five minutes. Try this afternoon.'

In the afternoon I was greeted by a subdued giggle.

'Here is that Englishman again. Surely he knows no one can ever contact the mayor.'

I had to do the thing I was trying to avoid. Ask him to phone me! I knew how difficult it was speaking French on the phone. Face to face I could use sign language to help me out. On the phone I was doubtful whether I could make him understand. It seemed the only answer though, so I left my phone number.

Three days later I was contemplating life in the little room, when the phone rang.

'It's the mayor,' confided Polly through the door.

Panic! My resolve crumbled.

'Can you deal with it?'

'He wants to speak to you.'

I'd had no time to concoct my opening gambit.

'You know what I want to ask him.'

'You're the one who wants to speak French.'

This hit home hard. I arrived at the phone, less than calm

and controlled, and began speaking in a slow, ponderous manner. I will have to admit, though, that after the third time of repeating something, my sentences did become much more fluent. However laborious the conversation might have been, I had managed to communicate and gain a reply. He suggested I try an old people's home in Moncontour. I was inwardly jubilant. My triumph was only slightly tempered by the fact that Denise, a guest and language teacher, had found it necessary to get up and leave the room, half-way through the conversation.

Sister Pierre was my contact at the *maison de retraite*. She was calm and gentle and made me think I would feel comfortable working under her direction. She asked about me, talked of her old people's home and the hospital in Lamballe, a place that I should try in my quest to do voluntary work. I left, pleased that I had taken part in such a lengthy conversation and that we had got on so well. It was not until later, I realized, that I had been rejected as being suitable to work in her home.

I had difficulties at the enquiry desk of Lamballe Hospital. They could not believe that I wanted to work without being paid. Eventually I was ushered into the office of one of the hospital administrators.

We talked for just under an hour (his work schedule must have been severely disrupted). His level of English was about on a par with my French. We both spoke with a peculiar mixture of the two, depending on the complexity of our intended remarks. We also helped each other out when in difficulties. It was a true team effort.

He took down my particulars, in order that I should do voluntary work. But this was a slow process, as he wanted to tell me about his children and how they were progressing with their private, English lessons. The forms and whether he wanted me seemed more and more irrelevant, as we became engrossed in an in-depth conversation on learning languages. Eventually the forms were completed, and a promise was given to ask the *directeur* about my most unusual request.

He was true to his word and permission was granted. I was asked to meet Madame Henri, in charge of services, at an appointed time, to make arrangements for involvement to begin.

Madame Henri was small, yet robust, with strong, bushy

eyebrows, which moved venomously with her every word. She was obviously on the work face, as I was accorded a hurried four minutes of her time. After two minutes of attempting to talk in her language, she stared at me, rearranged her eyebrows and told me that my French was not good enough. The patients were very fragile and I would be a liability. I suggested working in the kitchens, cleaning, anything, but it was to no avail. I was not required.

Rejection as a voluntary worker! This must surely be considered the epitomy of true failure in the history of job search. It did cross my mind, though, that going from one establishment to another, asking to do voluntary work, might be an excellent way of learning the language.

There were one or two other occasions when my ego was dented as a result of poor language skills. Before going to the hairdresser's, I had privately practised the difference between *chevaux* and *cheveux*, and so was confident I would not return with a style resembling a horse's mane. '*Court* – short or brief' had also been included in my word list, the day before. I felt well-prepared.

On entering the salon, I was immediately introduced to my hairdresser, a young woman with an enthusiastic sparkle in her eye. She led me to a chair, had my arms through a protective smock and my head back over the sink in no time at all. Then with vigorous confidence, she washed my hair and seated me in another chair, ready for action. 'Time and motion' would have been impressed.

Now was the time to indicate my precise requirements.

'*Un peu plus court*,' I suggested.

Being a little unsure how correct this phrase was, I reinforced this statement by using my thumb and forefinger, to show how little I wanted off. Three cuts of the scissors into mid-air was all the warm-up she needed, before she attacked my locks. A flurry of energetic speed followed. In the mirror I could see her frown of concentration, the scissors scything through my hair and more importantly the length of the fallen strands, as they rested on my shoulder. It was evident that my communication skills had not been adequate, for the amount I had wanted taking off was the amount left on my head. Whether it was because I felt unable to argue in French, or because readjustment of the length of my hair was a technical impossibility, I don't know. Either way I allowed her eager scissors to continue unimpeded. On completion, she took in a deep breath (I had never realized before that the cutting of hair constituted anaerobic exercise). She then admired her creativity. All I could do was inwardly bemoan the fact that now I had no chance to disguise my impending baldness.

My family's remarks were not over-complimentary. Luke giggled behind his hand. Kate mumbled some comment about an alien, and Polly raised an eyebrow and then considered the benefits of single beds in a nearby catalogue.

French numbers, to my surprise, caused one or two uncomfortable moments. I knew one to a hundred in French, as a result of monotonous learning by rote when at school. So I felt confident in dealing with most amounts required to pay for my shopping. In actuality my confidence was misplaced.

I had gathered together half a dozen items at the local supermarket and had brought them to the till. While the cost of them was being totted up, I was studiously sorting through a handful of money, as my coin identification had a lot to be desired. My deliberations were interrupted by the manager mentioning the sum I owed. He did this, not in a slow and clear manner, but in a blur. The only word I detected was *vingt*. Or was it *francs*? I wasn't sure. Quick thinking was needed. I closed my hand over my French money and stuffed it back into my pocket. Then I produced my saviour, the hundred franc note. This method of producing well over the amount needed, held me in good stead for a couple of weeks, though the strain of the change in my pockets was considerable.

I found that even if I could determine the sum asked for I still needed to translate it into English. This took time. The best approach seemed to be to forget the last number mentioned, which would probably be the centimes. Instead I tried to concentrate on the first number, the francs. This seemed to work and after a month or two only large sums of money caused any real problems.

Telephone numbers proved a similar difficulty. While talking to a potential squash partner, I was asked for my telephone number. He held paper and pen ready to jot it down.

'No problem,' I thought, '96.42.62.40.'

Unfortunately my recall of French numbers was not spontaneous.

'*Quatre-vingts* is eighty.' Therefore ninety is *quatre-vingts-dix – onze – douze – treize – quatorze – quinze – seize.*'

'*Quatre-vingt-seize*,' I said, preparing to work out what forty-two was in French.

Before I could continue, he passed me his paper and pen to write down the number for him.

Perhaps my most ignominious public failure took place at the ice rink. Polly had successfully changed our shoes for skates, but unfortunately Kate's skates were slightly too small. A thirty-four was needed rather than a thirty-three. I seized the skates and went to the desk to ask the attendant, a boy of no more than thirteen or fourteen, if I could change them. I placed the skates on the counter, looked at the boy and completely froze. I couldn't muster a word, only an inane smile.

'Thirty-two or thirty-four?' he said, in most presentable English.

'Thirty-four,' I said.

The rest of the conversation was also in English. I was crestfallen! I managed to maintain my spirits, though, by vehemently decrying my public school education while skating aggressively around the rink.

My most substantial setback came after about six weeks in France. I had just put the phone down after talking to a squash friend and was congratulating myself that the conversation had gone well, when Kate interrupted my thoughts.

'I speak better French than you do already,' she remarked.

'Yes, you probably do!' I replied, smiling condescendingly. 'I must encourage her. This is a good sign. She's gaining confidence every day.'

'You don't even say *une* properly. You say *yune*,' she continued.

She was right. In order to get that beautiful 'u' sound, I did put a 'y' in front of the 'u'. But surely everyone said it like that. I turned to Polly.

'It's pronounced *yune*, isn't it?'

'No, it is *une*.'

I was visibly shocked. I had been saying it wrongly all my French-speaking life.

When seen to have a fault or weakness, it seems to be human nature to blame somebody else. I was no exception in this respect. So rather than complimenting my daughter on her sharpness of ear and critical awareness, I morosely reflected on my two French teachers. Perhaps they too had learned their French from Mr Whitmarsh and had never stepped foot in France. Whatever the reason I had to lay the blame with them. I continued to do so until I managed to readjust my accent, something that took many months.

It was not until we had been in France for two and a half months that I noticed a change in the standard of my French. Up until then, despite my determination and Polly's reassurance, I could see no discernible difference in ability during that time. It was not until I had to make a trip to Britain that I could detect progress was being made. The ferry I travelled on had a French crew, and as a result all announcements were initially made in French. I found that I could understand what was being said without the aid of an English equivalent. I had never been able to do this before. I returned refreshed and eager to make further progress.

5

UNBRIDLED RELAXATION AND DEVIL-HORNED URGENCY

The renowned explosive French temperament can be seen at its worst behind the wheel of a car. That amiable 'after you' philosophy, which many British drivers possess is noticeably absent on the French roads. That cheery wave and grateful smile are usually replaced by steely seriousness and a total rejection of eye contact. French motorists regularly seem oblivious of others on the road, appearing to have just one aim in mind – reaching their destination.

I first realized the recklessness of many French motorists when part of a convoy of cars, transporting children to a sporting venue in Quessoy. The two cars in front soon started pulling away from me. I tried to keep in touch with as fast a piece of driving as I dared, but they quickly disappeared from view. Behind was the last member of the convoy. I had no idea where the stadium was, so I had two choices: continue and hope to come across it by chance or let the car behind overtake and try to follow her. I guessed that she might outpace me too, so I decided on the former option. My debating soon became irrelevant, as despite my efforts to maintain a fast rate of progress, she overtook me within a few hundred metres. She then slowed down to guide me to the sporting event.

It is not just the speed at which most French people drive, it is the danger that they put themselves in to do so. They have an almost hypnotic attraction for the car in front. Whether they want to overtake or not, they seem magnetized a few metres from the car ahead of them, impervious of what would happen if it had to brake. To encounter a French driver coming in the other direction on a narrow country lane can be a pulsating experience. It is like a game of chicken which a foreigner is assured of losing. My use of the grass verge has never been greater than in France. Two French car drivers negotiating a narrow road often consider the process as a sporting occasion. Both will drive down the middle of the road without reducing speed, until one submits, usually at the last moment, and veers towards the verge, so losing the contest. I expected to see more cars in ditches, but the French have put in a good deal of practice and have developed this activity into an art form.

The French people's approach to icy roads is also hair-raising. Their speed is diminished, but only marginally. There are many road signs in France which specifically warn drivers of black ice. This is very sensible, yet it almost seems below the dignity of the French to adjust their speed for mere supposition. Another well-practised phenomenon is to drive with just a porthole of visibility during frosty weather. At such times drivers can be seen with nose virtually touching windscreen, but with still no idea what is happening behind them or to either side.

On one occasion when Michel and I had finished playing squash we came from the courts to find our car windows had a thin layer of ice on them. I busily used my scraper on my windows, while Michel used his sleeve to create some sort of vision on the driver's side of his windscreen. I handed my scraper to him. He looked at it like a prehistoric man would, at someone's newly invented wheel.

He turned it over in his hands two or three times and politely nodded and grunted a muffled, 'Thanks.'

It was clear, though, that he did not know what to do with it, so I took it and did the job for him. More thanks followed, before he drove off with unbounded vision.

One of the better French habits is their use of indicators when wanting to overtake. On a winding road, to have an impatient indicator reminding you in the mirror, that someone behind is extremely keen to pass, can be disconcerting. It is better, though, than in Britain, where a couple of winks is often felt sufficient to describe your intent. In France the indicator often keeps flashing throughout the act of overtaking. On a dual carriageway some drivers will perpetually leave them on while staying in the outside lane. It may seem an ostentatious show of power yet it is of great assistance to other drivers. You know they're coming!

You would have thought that the French would be much more wary on the roads, given the reputation of the police. The police have the power of taking your licence from you on the spot and can prevent you continuing your journey, if you are travelling without it. In Britain it is only in extreme cases this will happen. You are also likely to have the relative comfort of a few months of being able to drive before you are given whatever ban you deserve. This is not the case in France. If it is an offence justifying loss of licence, the ban can begin immediately you have been stopped. Even so the rumour that you would lose the use of your car whatever your misdemeanour is a fallacy. My squash-playing friend, Michel, will testify to this as he was booked for speeding twice in one day.

I had already worked out my approach if the police stopped me for any reason. Like many British people, I was of the belief that if you feigned total incompetence at speaking the language, the police would be too exasperated to take up proceedings against you. This, together with the rigmarole of booking someone from a foreign country, was expected to deter any vigilant policeman from carrying out the letter of the law.

Whether my assumptions were correct or not was never put to the test. It was interesting to note, though, that on one of our trips back to England, the Plymouth security officers were stopping all cars with British number plates in order to inspect under the bonnet. Polly, concerned by the possibility of some form of terrorist act, enquired why it was only British cars that were being stopped.

The gruff reply was, 'The French don't speak English, do they?'

The time I was most likely to incur the wrath of the police, had I been in the vicinity, was the occasion I started driving as if I were in Britain. I had collected my *baguette* from a local bread shop and set off for home on the left-hand side. A few hundred metres ahead was a lorry coming in the other direction. As it approached, I began cursing the fact that French lorry drivers seemed to consider the middle of the road as their prerogative. Then I noticed that in fact the lorry did not straddle the middle of the road; instead it was on my side. It was not until the lorry flashed me, that I woke from my reverie and veered towards legality.

Our one involvement with the police was to report a theft.

One day I went to the boiler room to find that Justin's motorcycle was no longer there. While searching for it in our field I found a hiding place among some bushes, which had been flattened to create some form of resting place. In the middle of it lay Justin's leather jacket, which had been hanging in the boiler room. I left it where it was. Evidence! Fingerprints!

The next day Polly and I went to the police station. Rather than it being a stark, unpleasant place as I had imagined, it had a fairly friendly atmosphere. The policeman who greeted us certainly lacked that hostile grimace that my preconceived ideas had half-expected. Polly explained about the motor-bike and the coat.

He listened patiently and then said, 'Is it a *moto-becane* or a *solex*?'

We looked at each other for inspiration. None came.

'What's the vehicle identification number?'

The same look brought the same response.

'I'll need the vehicle identification number.'

A phone call to Justin was obviously necessary. We left feeling a little stupid, but while we were there we had gleaned that a *moto-becane* had been found abandoned in a ditch about two kilometres from our house. He also had given us a full description of it.

When we got home Polly found a receipt of purchase in one of the drawers. It was the same *moto-becane*. I had been slightly disappointed that the police had not decided to scrutinize the scene of the crime, so I decided to fetch the jacket from its sheltered spot. On picking it up. I noticed a Turtle badge pinned to the lapel. I called the children. This place had been one of their dens. They had been using the jacket in one of their games and had forgotten to return it. My disappointment at not being able to show my 'find' to the police suddenly vanished.

We had expected that the receipt would not be enough to reclaim the *moto-becane*. After all it would be so easy to fill in the information the police had already given us on a fresh receipt. Even so we decided to try. Again we got a warm reception. The receipt was thought to be adequate and the moto-becane was ours to take away. The policeman helped us put it in the back of the hatchback and searched successfully for some string to secure it. He was like an old-fashioned British bobby, not only in his manner, but also in the way he used his common sense rather than follow the normal formalities. Neither was 'correct procedure' the method he used to try and catch the thief. Instead he asked if we would contact our neighbours as to whether they had seen or heard anything.

* * *

To the French, meetings are very important, as they are the essence of community spirit and activities. Indeed they are often seen as an excuse for a social event. We participated in one very early in our stay.

Allen and Denise were visiting us when the school had its first parent/teacher meeting of the year. They happily volunteered to baby-sit, so that both of us could go. Having attended PTA meetings in Britain, I suggested that it would take no more than two hours, and said, as we were due to begin at 7.30, that we would be back by 10.30 at the latest. We arrived at the given time to find but one person there.

It was one of our first encounters with the French inclination to start activities later than the appointed time. In the primary school, children might be asked to play an extra ten or fifteen minutes at the beginning of the school day. Even on television the news would regularly over-run, making all the following programmes much later than advertised. There would be no hue and cry about this. Serious discussion is far more important than whether frivolous programmes are being screened on time. At first I found this annoying but after a while I became used to it. It was just an example of French people's relaxed, unhurried approach to their social lives.

The meeting began (thirty minutes later than scheduled) with the chairperson handing in her resignation. She added that the meeting would not continue unless a new chairperson were appointed. She then started to explain what the job entailed.

As she spoke her eyes moved from person to person, though occasionally her gaze rested on an individual for a few seconds. Then she would pointedly, yet softly, ask whether he or she would take on the position. She relied on the hypnotic ability of her grey-blue eyes, rather than any persuasive, verbal patter. Her stony stare was to no avail, though, as each person she asked managed to avert her eyes and give a more plausible reason for refusing the job. They couldn't afford the time, their parents were sick and needed looking after, there were problems with the roof of the house. A young-looking parent, who had been bright and eager throughout, declined as his child had only just started in the infant class. He knew little enough of the area, let alone what was happening in the school. The chairperson's piercing eyes did get him to volunteer his services on the committee, though. No one actually said they did not want to do the job, emphasizing what terrible luck it was that there were so many extenuating circumstances.

Polly and I eventually realized that, apart from late-comers, we were the only two who had not been asked. I started envisaging myself as the new, non-French speaking chairperson of the PTA, particularly as my answer to a question I could not understand was invariably a reflex action *oui*.

The chairperson stood her ground and refused to start the meeting without a new appointment. A different solution was proposed. The committee would meet separately and elect someone, whether they liked it or not. So the half a dozen members of the committee, together with the enthusiastic newcomer, went to another room. Twenty minutes later they reappeared with its rather bemused, new member elected as its chairperson.

It was now that the meeting could begin, just over an hour and a half after its scheduled start. The teachers (all were present, including a supply teacher) and parents were then embroiled in intense, energetic debate. Time seemed an irrelevance. Our interest in the proceedings began to diminish considerably.

While talking about school transport . . .

'We've got to go soon. They'll be wondering what on earth's happened.'

'We can't go before the food and drink.'

Wine and food had been promised towards the end of the meeting. The thought of our first French-style buffet had been most appetizing. As a result we had only had a light snack before going out.

While talking about the inclusion of swimming in the school day . . .

'No one will notice if we slip out.'

'We can't go yet, no one else has left.'

While talking about the weighty problem of whether the school water had caused a recent sickness virus . . .

'They'll be phoning the hospitals, the police.'

'If the "English" are seen to go before the food, they'll dismiss us as having no interest.'

The meeting seemed to be drawing to a close when the mayor entered. This revitalized the discussion and the women who had gone to organize the food and drink returned to their seats.

Eventually a very palatable wine was poured into plastic cups and slices of Madeira cake (such as you would never see in a *pâtisserie*) were offered round. On tasting the cake, I assessed that it could have been of similar vintage to the wine. Our first French buffet was a distinct disappointment, and our naive belief that the French did everything in style was shattered.

The refreshment did not mean the end of the meeting, though, for vigorous debate continued. It was at about ten to twelve that the first rumblings of movement to leave were made.

Having arrived home an hour and a half later than expected, Allen revealed some of the thoughts in his mind during our absence. They ranged from 'How do we contact the hospitals to see if they've been in an accident?' to 'What do we do with the children?' and 'Who on earth does the house belong to?'

The feeling of isolation in a foreign country, when a problem arises, was truly emphasized. In future we would have to forego trying to promote reputations of being solid, supportive citizens.

Outside the school I had already passed the time of day with many of the parents who were at the PTA meeting. To say *bonsoir* and *ça va* a dozen times in the space of five minutes, in many ways may seem a little tedious and meaningless. Yet it is an accepted necessity when greeting someone in France and should not be belittled. It is another sign of that togetherness which is one of the strengths of the French community. Such etiquette can only open the way to knowing more people and as a result having the opportunity to widen your group of friends.

I thought my presence at the PTA meeting would enhance my chances of greater conversational contact with these people. At first it proved not to be so. I had to find a reason for this, other than my reluctance to practise my clumsy French in their company. My answer was to blame the PTA meeting.

In trying to read these parents' thoughts, I imagined them subconsciously thinking, 'He would have to be an idiot to sit through a four hour meeting, only being able to understand the odd word here and there. He must have a good command of French. If that's the case why on earth doesn't he say something more than just, *bonsoir*? He must be one of those aloof Englishmen. If that's the case, why should I bother?'

These thoughts obviously arose from my paranoia, though I still feel there was a strand of truth in my meanderings. For a long time I found discussion at the school gate difficult.

Remarkably a change seemed to come about as a result of some of the French children's reactions to me. They appeared to take to me as they had to Kate and Luke. They would talk to me simply and slowly, naturally realizing that I had similar language difficulties as my two children. I had stood in British primary school playgrounds mostly getting no more than a half-smile from children I knew quite well. In France I was having conversations with children I hardly knew.

One of the most unforgettable moments of my stay was the first time I received a traditional French kiss. It was from a little seven-year-old girl, Marie. She stood in front of me, her head in line with my waist.

'*Bonsoir*, Peter,' she said, looking up at me, with her dark, innocent eyes.

She stretched her neck towards me and at the same time turned her cheek. I hesitated for a moment, but still her expectant cheek was raised towards me. I leant forward to kiss her. I was touched. To Marie it meant nothing more than the English equivalent of 'glad to see you'. The only people I kissed like that were either very good friends or ancient aunts. To me that kiss was a sign of genuine warmth from a child and a symbol of the start along the road towards acceptance within the community. The fact that I had to ask Kate and Luke what the girl's name was, only emphasized the effect of the greeting.

This contact with children was a lead for some of their parents to begin talking to me. Emile's mother, Madelaine, was the first to break the conversational barrier. While we spoke, it was interesting to note three other parents sidle up to us. They were talking to each other, though there were noticeably long pauses between bouts of conversation. They were evidently eager to glean any gossip-worthy information about my reasons for being in Moncountour. Eventually nearly every parent was willing to communicate. (This was in direct contrast to my experiences in British playgrounds. Only a few parents would forward a 'hello', let alone participate in animated discussion.) There were, though, three notable exceptions. They would pointedly avoid my gaze, and even if our children were friendly with theirs, they could not even muster a *bonsoir*. To them we were infiltrators.

Two parents spoke to me in English outside the school gates, though their approaches to me were markedly different. One mother's opening gambit was in English. She was a flamboyant person, whose sentences ran wild and contained a highly imaginative use of tense. She loved to use the language and I became her reciprocating puppet. She did perhaps try to impress the other parents, but it was also a means of practice, something she was rarely able to do. The other mother, seeming intuitive to my needs, did not reveal she spoke English for two or three weeks.

It was only when I had stuttered to a halt, trying to explain some complex idea, that she quietly interjected with, 'I can speak English if you wish.'

We developed a good understanding and only spoke English when I found things too difficult. She was very supportive in my attempt to improve my own language skills.

There is a mythical belief that the vast majority of French people can speak at least some English. This idea comes from British people's experiences while on holiday. It is a false concept, for the French people they are likely to meet will need English to hold down any job which involves much contact with tourism. Outside this tourist sphere, people's knowledge of English is sparse. Ninety per cent of the parents I talked with possessed a negligible amount of English.

What one or two of them did say, though, was, 'I can't speak English but my teenage children . . .'

* * *

In most of France people's love of food has led to them considering the lunchtime period as sacrosanct. It is only in large cities that the tradition is not so widespread. A Macdonalds in a city is a fair indication that time-honoured eating habits are being eroded.

Brittany certainly comes to a halt between 12.30 and 2.00. It is the time that Bretons indulge in this hallowed culinary ritual, which is seldom hurried and defies interruption. To make a commercial contact during lunch-hour would be futile and to telephone a family in the middle of their meal could verge on the insolent. The French telephone system between 12.30 and 1.30 is rarely used for business calls and is designated as a cheap-rate period.

I visited a large supermarket in Lamballe at one o'clock. It was virtually deserted. As I came to pay for my shopping, instead of the normal, lengthy queues, there was only a bored looking cashier (the one person apparently on duty in the store) to greet me. Her head lolled lazily to one side. Her unsmiling face bore all the signs of someone whose turn it was to endure the hardship of a delayed lunch-break.

On another occasion Polly and I had gone to Dinard Airport, to book a flight for a relative. We arrived at 12.25. The woman produced that customary, welcoming smile.

'Can I help you?'

'I'd like to book a flight.'

'Where to?'

'Bristol.'

This last word caused the ground hostess a certain amount of subdued agitation. To travel to Bristol involved two flights. It would take about a quarter of an hour to process everything.

'Can you come back at two o'clock?'

'Sorry, we've got to be elsewhere at two.'

'The computer's down.'

'But you don't close till half past.'

'But it's my lunch-hour. I don't get another break until this evening.'

At last the truth was out. It was a *mauvaise heure*. Lunch was going to be affected. She had become more and more flustered in her attempts to forego dealing with us. It seemed that if she were not regaled at the normal time, withdrawal symptoms might occur. Having run out of cogent arguments, she became resigned to the fact that her lunch-break would be shorter than usual, and her previous calm returned as she processed the tickets. Even so the magnetic smile, which was so evident when we arrived, had become a watery replica.

'To work hard and play hard' could well describe the philosophy of the French. I would prefer the maxim to have the word 'play' replaced by 'relax'.

6

THE HUNTER AND THE HUNTED

Arachnophobia was luckily not a problem in our household. Had it been, an extermination programme would have had to be put into action from the day we arrived. I am certain that if our house lay untouched for a year a veil of webs would encompass every room. As it was, for a while we left the spiders to roam freely, though at the same time, paradoxically destroyed their attractive homes. We suffered from that inbuilt conditioning which suggested that any sign of a spider's web indicated an uncleaned house. Occasionally one of us might be surprised by one of the larger spider's presence, though the shock would never send us into a fit of stamping rage. Two monstrous ones appeared in our bedroom sink from time to time, but there was never the urge to wash them away into oblivion.

Our attitude to spiders changed after Keith and Annita visited us. On the first night with us, Keith retired early to his bed in the dungeon. The following evening Keith's account of what had happened was dramatic.

He was greeted by a large spider in the middle of the floor. He skirted the room, clambered on the nearest bed and removed one shoe. All the time he kept his eyes firmly fixed on the spider. With shoe in hand, he reached out his arm to a position where he could flatten this beastly foe. He clung to the side of the bed to ensure he did not overbalance and have to grapple with the evil creature. His first aim was true and effective. Even so five more blows were felt necessary to extinguish any discernible murmur of life that might exist. He then clumsily and quickly undressed for bed. From under the protection of the duvet, his eyes searched every corner of the room for any signs of concerned relatives.

Annita then continued the story. She had entered the dungeon to find Keith, with eyes wide open, tightly cocooned in his duvet. He had even tucked the counterpane underneath him.

'What on earth are you doing, Keith?'

'A spider!' he retorted, pointing at the dark, flat blob in the middle of the room.

'Yes, but it's dead, Keith.'

'They often go around in pairs, you know.'

When Keith and Annita had gone out for the day, I decided to decimate our spider population in the cause of human harmony. In future, when visitors were imminent, cleaning the house meant killing the spiders, as well as the other duties.

My confidence in dealing with spiders was slightly eroded one day, when doing the ironing. As I picked up a pair of trousers, a large spider started crawling down one of the legs. I placed the trousers on the ironing board and raced for my camera. I was about to take a picture but decided that its position on the bottom of my trousers did not do justice to its size. I ruffled them, to try and move it to a place where its most imposing features could be displayed. It immediately shot round the other side and out of view. I rushed round, camera at the ready, but it was nowhere to be seen. I investigated further, but it had disappeared. It must have gone up the trouser leg and found some dark crevice in which to hide!

Although spiders don't bother me, the thought of one wandering around inside a pair of trousers I was wearing was a little distressing. I vigorously shook the trousers. Still no spider! I cautiously peered inside. No sign! There was a pile of washing in the basket on the floor. Each garment was inspected thoroughly. This camera-shy creature had truly vanished.

Three days later I came to wear the same trousers. I had to turn them inside out before I was satisfied that it was not still deviously crouching there.

Flies were definitely a 'bug-bear'. An entourage of flies invariably accompanied the fresh air that was allowed in to relieve the stuffy atmosphere in the house. If they were disinclined to leave via the same route, their chances of a long life were seriously diminished. A slow painful death was assured by our electric fly-killing contraption, though more traditional methods were used when unmolested tranquillity was required. Use of the rolled newspaper was fairly efficient, though it did necessitate the more frequent cleaning of window panes.

A forceful swish of the wrist was, of course, the most common method of giving immediate relief from the flies' irritating habits. It seldom cured the problem, though. I now understand why cows are so patient when flies are perpetually hovering around their eyes. After numerous hand-flicking attempts to dishearten them from being annoying, a form of lethargic submission can set in, and you simply let them have their nagging way.

Other infiltrators into our domain were black ants. Hundreds could be seen scurrying around the outside of our house. They seemed ever aware of our presence and only spasmodically intruded. There were the occasional raids to explore the potential of a spilt drink or to carry off a crumb of biscuit. One muscular cheese carrier's life was even given a reprieve, as I found his feats of strength an interesting phenomenon.

On other occasions squadrons of ants delved into enemy territory in an attempt to overrun areas of the house. The first time this occurred, Jon and Liz were occupying the downstairs bedroom. As I was cleaning the fireplace, I heard persistent stamping noises emanating from their room. Initial thoughts were of an early morning fitness drive. But Jon soon came out to tell me that there were hundreds of ants in the room (he was exaggerating, there were only about one hundred). Jon's trusty, size enormous shoe had already accounted for many of the intruders. A can of anti-ant spray, which was in residence when we arrived, accounted for the rest.

With wild life all around us it was not surprising that we came to consider some of the animals who lived near us as our friends. Their feelings about us probably reached no further than that we were trespassing on their property. Even so their frequent or intermittent presence endeared them to us.

Two small, green lizards could often be seen sunbathing on one of the rocks or flitting from one log to another outside the dungeon. Neither had a complete tail, both having left them behind in an unlucky predator's mouth. One nearly lost more than its tail on one occasion. I had sliced a log in two with mallet and chisel and had begun sawing one of the halves, when the vibrations made the loose bark fall from the log. Clinging to the wood beneath was one of our bright-green friends. When I had split the wood and started sawing, it had not moved, despite the fact that these actions must have seemed like an earthquake to a tiny lizard. Even when its hiding place had been revealed it stayed like a statue, either through sheer fright or because it really believed it was still concealed. I gently placed both lizard and log on the rocks. The log was not burnt that night. When I came to saw the log again a few days later, it went through a thorough inspection before I allowed the saw's teeth to rasp into the wood.

A more ostentatious lizard revealed itself to us after I had met Kate and Luke at the school gate one evening. On returning to the car, there was a lizard residing on the passenger seat. Earlier in the day I had loaded the car with stray, fallen branches from the roadside, in order to bolster our depleted supply of logs. The lizard must have decided that its bark hiding place was insecure, and had sought refuge in the nooks and crannies of our car. It created the expected interest at first. But when I suggested it should join the other lizards at home, Luke realized he would have to travel in the car with this animal, that could be crawling over him while he was powerlessly strapped in by his seat belt. The lizard had to be removed.

Have you ever tried to get a lizard out of a car? I could see myself chasing it for the next hour or so. My first thought was to try and catch it. I rejected this immediately as I did not like the idea of being left with a wriggling tail. In addition I felt that a lizard half its original length would be twice as difficult to remove. I had resolved to flick it out of the open car door, though I expected it to be far too quick for my hand. Before I had attempted this operation, it had placed its front feet on a copy of *Libération*, lying next to it on the seat. I decided to push the rest of the newspaper under its body, so being able to eject it much less harshly. Having pushed the paper under half of the lizard's body, I lifted it in the hope that, although two legs would be dangling, the lizard would still be balanced on it. My assessment seemed awry, as its body started slipping back to the seat. Luckily it completed the task for me by clambering onto the paper. So our intruder, with the assistance of the aptly named newspaper, was gently placed near a hedge, allowing us to return home untroubled.

I could not help thinking that our move to France was far less traumatic than the lizard's rehabilitation. It had been wrenched involuntarily from family and home and placed in a completely strange habitat, where there might not even have been another of its kind for miles.

There was one of the herd of cows in the field next to us who seemed more inquisitive about our behaviour than the others. Her full, black face would, more often than not, be seen chomping the delights of our hedge and at the same time looking in our bedroom window as we opened our shutters of a morning. Her most distinguishing feature was a headband of tassled rope. As she was one of the stouter members of the herd, I surmised that she did not wear it to accentuate her athletic prowess. Neither was it a form of fashion-conscious vanity. Her change of headwear for a far less becoming tangle of wire indicated that she had a problem with her stubby horns.

The dogs who, untended, would pass through our property were gentle beasts once they had accepted our presence. We did not, however, befriend the Siamese cat who would lurk in the bushes in search of adventure. It was his prey that we preferred.

Before arriving in France my knowledge of birds was minimal. It was restricted to being able to identify only common British garden birds and even those became difficult to spot at a distance. A bird over fifty metres away became somewhere between grey and black in colour, totally indistinguishable. I had always blamed colour blindness for this inability, though deep down I knew that I simply had not taken the time and trouble to look and learn. There had always been an inner wish to know more about birds, so I had come to France armed with a glossy bird book.

La Ville Méen was surrounded by birds. A flock of sparrows nested near the house. They seemed to have some sort of affinity with the cows, for they did much of their feeding in their field. They would only leave when the cows disappeared to be milked. Regularly at six o'clock they would return to the house, as their compatriots swung their way up the drive to the milking shed. The sparrows would cluster among the vines in animated discussion about the day's adventures.

A robin, in whose territory our house lay, was a regular visitor. He was a bold individual who would happily watch us eat breakfast from the window sill. He even dallied in our bedroom a couple of times, when the French windows had been left open.

His bravery on one occasion nearly lost him his life. Kate went to the dungeon to get out her bike (the dungeon was used as a bike shed when we had no visitors). She surprised the robin, who had flown through the door that had been left ajar. He flew full tilt at the room's only window. It was some eight feet from the floor and closed. He dropped like a stone landing on his back. Kate rushed to me, distraught. When I reached the dungeon, the robin was still in the same position, lifeless. I went to get some newspaper which was to be the bird's coffin. When I came back the robin had got to its feet. He shivered in the corner in stunned bewilderment. His eyes blinked like a cricketer adjusting to the light or, more aptly, a boxer, having risen from the canvas, focussing on the next punch. Gone was his cock-sure confidence. He was a shrivelled, unkempt shadow of his former self. Kate shrewdly fetched some birdseed and scattered it between the robin and the now wide-open door. We then went for a walk and happily found the robin had gone on our return.

When I was going to fetch the newspaper I had wondered whether it was possible to practise artificial resuscitation on a bird. The Holger-Nielsen method, using wings instead of arms, was a little far-fetched and mouth-to-mouth would have presented insurmountable difficulties. But could you not place a plastic tube in the bird's mouth and blow through the other end or softly tap its chest to try and revive its heart? The thought of applying these medical initiatives hastened my decision that the bird must be dead.

The following morning I looked hopefully out of the window for signs of the robin. I was not disappointed. He was his assured self again. I had had thoughts of him suffering from secondary shock or, in his dazed state, walking into the open jaws of a grateful predator. Had the robin perished in our dungeon, could the fact that he had flown into a man-made piece of glass have meant that he died of natural causes?

A perky-tailed wren was another indoor visitor. He also had once flown into the dungeon and, on being disturbed, was unable to find the exit. As with the robin, a suitable time was given for him to find his way out, and when I returned there was no sign of him. I locked the room.

Three days later I gave the room a breath of fresh air and was surprised by the wren shooting straight past me, out through the door. This was obviously a planned move; after all he had had plenty of time to consider his escape route. This non-paying guest had left his mark on the room (or more appropriately, marks). His droppings were on the bikes, the floor, the carpet, the beds and the top of the wardrobe, where he had probably concealed himself originally. I had to dive for my precious bird book to find what wrens eat: insects and spiders. Our attempts to rid the dungeon of all creatures that would upset guests had evidently not been a total success. Indeed the wren had departed very powerfully, leaving no suggestion of being near to starvation.

One of the pair of great tits proved to be a very likeable character. Like the robin he would come close to the house in search of food. In the winter, though, he showed a more fearless, even arrogant side to his personality. He would cling to part of the window frame and aggressively tap four or five times on the pane. He was obviously indignant that we should be sitting in relative warmth while he had to stay out in the cold, with a mere handful of feathers to cover him.

As a novice bird-watcher, the rarer visitors gave me most delight. My method of using binoculars in one hand and colourful bird book in the other, to try and identify a bird, might be scorned by the professional ornithologist, yet it helped me spot a few species I had never knowingly seen before. I saw a striking stonechat, a willow warbler (I think), migrating fieldfares and redwings and a short-toed tree-creeper. You may marvel at me being able to tell the difference between a normal tree-creeper and a short-toed one, as they look so similar. My trusty book gave me the answer: there are no ordinary tree-creepers in Brittany, just the short-toed variety. The colourful pigeon turned out to be a jay. He would inspect our field very timidly, before departing elsewhere, having sensed a human presence.

Another friend of more menacing proportions was a kestrel. I have often seen kestrels hovering near a motorway, happy only to be near humans and their cars, because the vehicle vibrations attract such an immense number of vermin. Never, though, had I seen their beauty at close quarters. Occasionally this kestrel would drift over the cow field, but normally she would be positioned, like a sentinel, on a wire fence or post near a lane leading to the main road. As we passed she would usually take to flight, but not before she had shown off her proud speckled chest.

Our favourite guest in the field was a male pheasant, with his bold, dark green and red head and audacious white stripe on the back of his neck. These strong colours seemed a stubborn, outward show of defiance to any would-be hunter. He arrived with us in late November, having almost certainly been chased there by the hunters. He would sometimes be seen around the fringes of the gravel area, arrogantly sniffing the air or inspecting the ground. Even so he would mostly hide in the bushes and undergrowth surrounding our field, his presence being only given away by a distinctive 'caw-caw' from time to time. We became protective towards him, contemplating distractions for the hunters who were still plying their trade at weekends, despite it being a good number of weeks since the start of the season.

Early one Sunday morning we were woken by hounds barking. The high-pitched noise intensified as they drew nearer. We could now hear the excitable shouts of the hunters. We then heard five rifle shots in quick succession. A sixth followed shortly after. The noises diminished.

Our pheasant had obviously escaped again, for we saw him no more.

In France the whole community has a completely different attitude to hunting than in Britain. The British tend to be discreet about having an interest in the sport. When they are in the company of other known hunters, their stories and descriptions are often vivid and told with voracious enthusiasm, but the fear of outraged neighbours or even animal rights activists is enough to persuade them not to hang what they have shot outside their front door.

The French, on the other hand, are generally a nation of red-blooded meat eaters and are proud of their hunting traditions. The *boucherie* will openly display animals in their unbutchered state, as an attraction to customers. The British butcher is more likely to have his meat cut and ready for purchase, it having little resemblance to the original. Those I have talked to who have never hunted before, have shown a wish to do so. I have never encountered a French person who admits to anti-hunting inclinations.

Whenever I had mentioned that we had left our red setter with friends in Britain their reaction was not, 'Oh what a lovely dog!' Instead their response was, 'Does she hunt?'

To visit the home of a Frenchman who owns hounds will quite likely lead to being introduced to them shortly after your arrival. Manuella's father was one such owner. His pride in his dogs became immediately apparent as he showed them to me within two minutes of first meeting him.

One dog had only one eye. He described in vivid detail how a fox had caused this loss. His description, told with passion, was accompanied by a dramatic improvisation of the event. This included the dog sniffing the ground, the snapping of jaws and the slow and decisive shaking of the head with clenched teeth, to indicate the death of the fox. It was a fine performance, which underlined his love for the dogs and the sport.

La chasse, c'est la nature! was a sticker in a car's rear window. It sums up the vast majority of French people's approach to hunting. The bird will seek the worm; the human will seek the bird (at any rate the ones he considers palatable). We are all hunters and such instincts should not be suppressed! To disagree would be unusual. If you do not want the hunters to practise their sport on your land, you must write to the *mairie* each year the season starts and your wishes will be expressed in the local newspapers. There are no thoughts that the process should be reversed, and that you should ask permission to hunt on people's land. Some acquaintances were talking of the fact a hunter had recently killed another by mistake. Their interesting reaction was not of shock or sympathy but that it was 'all part of the sport'. Hunting is definitely in the Frenchman's blood.

The start of the hunting season came to us as an abrupt surprise. We expected a quiet, lazy Sunday morning. Instead there was a mass of activity. Hatchbacks and estate cars littered the countryside, many with rear doors left wide open, presumably because of their owner's eagerness to hunt. In their hard-wearing clothes, that gave a suggestion of camouflage, these hunters were scattered over the fields, their guns ever at the alert. Beagles, basset hounds or dogs of similar ilk could be seen weaving in and out of hedges and long grass, doing the necessary detective work for their masters. It seemed impossible for any creature to escape this intense, almost systematic scouring of the countryside on the very first day. Yet, it was obvious that those who had cheated the hunters' bullet last year had learnt enough cunning to outfox their most deadly of foes, for throughout the season the echo of gunshot became a familiar sound.

My only feeble assistance to the beleaguered game came when driving towards Lamballe. On the main road was a female pheasant, stunned and disorientated. She had obviously not heard that hunters did not shoot the female of the species (unless through an unfortunate accident). Had she realized, she might well have stood her ground and ignored the aggressive barks and raucous cries emanating for her previous hall of residence. I stopped the car and shooed her still further away from her home, looking over my shoulder, like a dog protecting its dinner, in case a hunter might see my unholy act.

It felt uncomfortable to have total strangers tramping through our property, particularly when they all carried guns and had two or three dogs in tow. When it first happened I stood just outside the front door, expecting one of the men to apologize for the disturbance and ask if they could continue their search for game.

Instead I received a friendly, '*Bonjour!*'

When one of the dogs proceeded to cock its leg by one of the rose bushes, I waited for the apology and a sharp word to be given to the culprit. A cheery smile was the dog owner's sole response.

I pictured an English country garden, with its owner tending his beloved roses. In walked a stranger, with a dog at heel. The dog decided to urinate over the gardener's prize bush. I tried to imagine the gardener giving the stranger a jovial smile, the type I had given in response to the hunters. My image disappeared in the same way as a dream does when it gets to its most ludicrous point.

I had wanted to tell the hunters to get off my land (correction, Justin and John's land). I had wanted to tell them to leave the poor innocent animals alone. In Britain I would have probably gone part of the way towards doing that. In

France my uncertainties about the culture and inability to hold a reasonable conversation, let alone participate in a full-scale argument, persuaded me that my reply should be a smile.

After rushing inside for my camera, I managed to stop one of the hunters before he joined his compatriots, who had pushed their way through the hedge surrounding our field. We spoke for a short time about hunting. I found they were hoping for pheasant or rabbit. They had not seen a pheasant that day but they had discovered some rabbits. Even so they had failed to kill one, as the rabbits had inconsiderately disappeared into their burrows. While talking to me his voice possessed a high-pitched, nervous excitement. This reached a passionate crescendo when he talked of the rabbits' escape route. It seemed to me quite fair that the rabbits used their burrows to protect themselves from the barrage of shot which would have winged in their direction. He was adamant that it was most unreasonable and swore uninhibitedly at the existence of these burrows. He evidently would have preferred them to be lined up on their haunches in open ground, so he could shoot them like ducks at a fairground. I asked him if I could photograph him. He agreed, showing mock modesty. As I was about to take his picture, I could see him puff out his chest and push forward his chin. He was a true hunter.

During our conversation I had refrained from intimating my aversion to hunting. I thought about this afterwards and decided any pangs of conscience I had were merely a sign of hypocrisy. I can happily crush a spider or swat a fly, and I enjoy meats immensely, including horse. Therefore why should I become upset because animals which I happen to like, are being killed close to my home? I needed to develop the hardness of a true countryman.

Our neighbour, Monsieur Gilbert, is a staunch, unyielding man of the soil. In spite of his hardened exterior, he is a caring man. He tends his fields meticulously, finding time to prune the trees in his charge, something which gives him no economic reward. He must love his two alsatians for they obey his every whim, yet there is no sign of affection for them. There is no tasty, hand-fed morsel, no reassuring pat for these dogs. At night they are left outside (thankfully tethered) in all weathers. If one were to die, I am sure he would shed no tear. It would simply be the natural way of things. He would have seen

Nature at its cruelest and might well have watched a rainstorm decimate his harvest. I doubt, though, whether he would have stood to appreciate the rainbow that might have straddled the sky in the dying moments of the storm. The farming population outwardly appears unaffected by beauty and sympathy.

Despite the cold logic of my thoughts, I proved myself to be a true towny. I still disliked the idea of hunting. I would still cry incessantly at the death of one of my pets and I would still (as I did in Britain) fly out onto a balcony in near naked attire, to try and prevent a cat from attacking a nest full of blackbird fledglings.

'I wish that cow would stop mooing, it's putting me off my *boeuf bourgignon.*'

7

THE CRUNCH OF NIGHT

It was the night-time which proved to be particularly different from our previous town existence. We had been used to the sounds of traffic and passing people. We had never thought that these noises could be considered as reassuring contact with the outside world. But for the first two or three weeks of our venture, this was the case. At times the total and sustained silence in the country made us feel uncomfortable enough to maintain conversation, in order to hide the inactivity outside.

To encounter complete darkness was just as unnerving. When there was cloud cover and no outside light to guide the way, the inability to judge distance and direction was a new experience.

One night I had volunteered to rescue a number of forgotten clothes on the washing line. The bulb had gone in the outside light, so I endeavoured to follow the winding path to the line in darkness. The confidence I had in my sense of direction led me to stride manfully for the beginning of the path. My aim was awry, though, and I became ensnared by a prickly bush. On other occasions it may be interesting to ponder how easily a thorn will enter clothing yet will rip and tear its way out. Now was not the time for such considerations. I tried to release myself through gentle manipulation at first, quickly followed by a more frenzied approach to the problem. Angry impatience best describes my struggle with the bush, for having ripped my trousers, while unsubtly freeing myself from the thorns, I set off in the wrong direction. On hitting the charred remains of a bonfire, I soon realized I was further away from the washing line than when I had set out.

It was then I stopped to take in the situation. A momentary, clammy feeling of insecurity came over me. There was that need to touch something familiar. I had often blasphemed at the phosphorescent glare of a street lamp outside my bedroom window. This short time in total blackness must lead me to apologize for such profanities. I peered in every direction and as my eyes grew accustomed to the lack of light, the shapes of trees and the house were just visible against the sky. I staggered over the hummocks of grass towards my quarry. To touch the plastic washing line gave me a surprising feeling of relief. I felt my way along the line, releasing each item of clothing. I then returned, without further setbacks, to the house. On the way back I felt slightly aggrieved that the closed shutters had failed to give me a chink of assistance. In the cold of winter such disaffection did not exist, as I was thankful for their sturdy effectiveness.

The shutters' refusal to let light in or out, at first led to us feeling a little disorientated in the mornings. Gone was the build-up of rush-hour noise and light seeping through the curtains, helping us to grow accustomed to the idea of getting out of bed. On the day we first took the children to school we questioned the correctness of our alarm because it was so dark in our bedroom. There were no clues that day had dawned.

Total darkness in our bedroom at night, together with the lack of movement outside, led to one or two sleepless nights initially. The worst thing about silence is when it is broken. Every slight noise is noticeable. Before going to bed each tiny murmur would gain that stiff-necked, cocked-head reaction, which was supposed to enable us to listen more intently.

In the early hours of one morning during our first fortnight, my dreams of what would be were disturbed by the echoing sound of metal being banged.

A moment later, 'What was that?' filtered through unenthusiastically from beneath the duvet.

'I didn't hear anything,' I lied.

Total silence! Then, just as our bodies began to relax again, the same tinny noise reversed the process.

'The oil thieves!' I proclaimed.

'Go out and have a look!' Polly responded assertively.

Donning my short dressing gown to cover my nakedness did not appeal. Although the night was mild, I would have to step over an electric fence, jump a ditch and fight off a proliferation of brambles before encountering the oil tank. I felt decidedly unprotected.

'You must be joking!' I replied, failing to produce any form of persuasive logic to prevent Polly following her previous remark with:

'Just poke your head out of the door and see if anyone's about.'

Finding your dressing gown in complete darkness is no easy feat. I eventually found it, after pawing my way round the bedroom in the place I had first looked. I had not realized how much like a dishcloth the texture of my dressing gown felt. I picked up my keys and walked carefully to the front door, trying to remember where I had last put the mousetrap.

After rattling my keys loudly, I decided against looking outside. Instead I peered through the glass of the front door and scoured the total blackness for any sign of human life. Not surprisingly I saw no one. This convinced me that nobody was anywhere near the house. I returned to bed with added confidence.

'Did you go outside?'

'No.'

'But I heard footsteps on the gravel.'

'No, just me feeling my way around the house.'

'There were definitely footsteps outside.'

Polly bravely went to investigate. It was my turn to hear the crunch of gravel.

'Couldn't see anything!'

'That noise must have been you and I walking through the house.'

'We've got smooth tiles on the floor, not a ton and a half of gravel.'

Stubborn silence! That hollow, almost ghostly, metal sound interrupted it. It was repeated twice more in the next minute. Further tentative comments about the mystery followed, until an unspoken, mutual agreement was reached to use the duvet as a barrier against the unknown. This protection was sufficient for Polly, but I kept waiting for the next resounding tinkle. It kept coming at regular intervals.

The night brings out considerable creativity in people. Why should Polly send me out to meet a villainous gang of oil thieves who are armed to the teeth and ready to murder all who stand in their way? After questioning my wife's motives, I came up with the answer to our mystery. It wasn't oil thieves after all! The previous evening the neighbouring farmer had brought, by tractor, a wagon full of what at first glance looked like feed for the cows in the field next to us. He had emptied the wagon and tried unsuccessfully to cover it all with a large tarpaulin. Perhaps it wasn't feed but seed for the newly ploughed fields. It must be the farmer, one of his workers or his wife with a tin can banging it to frighten birds, mice and rats from devouring his seed. Being assured that my explanation was far safer than any other I had come up with, I slept.

The morning produced more banging of metal and the answer to the previous night's problem. One of the flaps of the wagon that had brought the seed, (sorry, feed) had been left unfastened. It was hitting the side of the wagon whenever a gust of wind caught it. Incidentally, detective work at a later date discovered that walking over a rush mat sounds exactly like walking on gravel.

The next night having solved the mystery, I seemed to be in the dream world of *déjà-vu*, for I was woken by a similar, husky, 'What was that?' from Polly.

I listened, heard nothing and with an incoherent splutter and a frown of annoyance turned over, only to hear a slight, rustling sound. The slight rustle gathered momentum until it became a frenetic scuffle of echo proportions.

'It's under the sink where the wastepaper basket is,' came Polly's wide-awake assessment of the situation.

A bloody mouse! Only the day before, for an instant, I had matched eyeball with eyeball with what was probably the same mouse, as it explored our lack of washing-up expertise in the crockery cupboard. He or she, or more popularly it, had scampered down two shelves and seemed to disappear into the shoe-cleaning box. (My reluctance to clean shoes was considerably reinforced in the next few days.) Definite munching could now be heard – munching, mark you, not nibbling.

'It's a big mouse or half a dozen of them.' Polly whispered.

'It's exactly the same noise as the Ryvita mouse made,' I said, lying trying to reassure myself as well as Polly.

It's funny how you keep your worst fears to yourself, as if frightened to display your own vulnerability. The word, 'RAT', had been emblazoned on my mind for at least thirty seconds. Action was required! I seized one of my shoes and flung it, hitting the wooden surround to the sink. There was silence, then the chomping continued, albeit more demurely. Undeterred, I felt for the other shoe and took careful aim at the curtain, shielding the wastepaper basket. A direct hit! Complete silence! I modestly congratulated myself of my prowess and determination, shrugging aside the cynical comment from Polly about welly-boot throwing competitions.

I know it was a successful operation, as I spent the next two and a half hours listening to see if it would return. I heard every creaking window and stretching beam, until the alarm rang to tell me it was time to wake up. A look at the mousetrap in the kitchen showed it still cocked, with Rocquefort cheese missing. A fine feast was had by all (not 'it' as it turned out). Incidentally, the French mouse is extremely patriotic, rejecting Edam and smuggled Cheddar for the joys of Brie and Rocquefort.

One word of warning: if you have a mouse colony, make sure your trap is out of hearing distance of your bedroom. That sharp crack of the metal bar will surely wake you from your slumbers as it did me. But it is not that which arouses the imagination. It is the resulting tussle which, in the largeness of night, leads to such thoughts as a rat trying to untangle its irritating mousetrap collar. Or alternatively, a mouse with a trap attached to its tail, trying to squeeze through those impossible cracks in vain.

I killed about fifteen mice during our stay. At first my success rate was not impressive. The mice would invariably ignore my trap and enjoy their banquet in some hidden corner. Eventually, after trial and much error, I seemed to uncover the secret. Previously I had placed the trap where the mouse had been seen or heard. A change of tactic proved more productive. I left the trap where the mouse had left its minute, dark droppings, the most frequent place being the floor of the toilet.

This seemed a peculiar area to search for food. Suggestions that they were developing a more human approach to their toiletry were dismissed. The probable reason for them using the room so often did not come to us until we were packing at the end of our stay. There was a pipe leading from the toilet under the stairs, where the box for our television was stored. The mice had gnawed their way into the box and created in vandalistic fashion some sort of play area. Our toilet and the gap made for the pipe were entry to the rooms where the panacea of our liberally sprinkled bread and biscuit crumbs lay.

The mice's culinary interests were not restricted to food. One mouse delighted in gnawing the flakier logs in the basket next to the fire. Another chewed around the edges of a pawn, accidentally left lying on the floor, rather than being returned to the cupboard with the rest of the chess pieces. Whether the mouse was gaining retribution on the pawn, blaming it for killing its distant cousin months previously, I do not know. The ruthless attack on the pawn was not quite terminal, though, for it remained part of the chess set, despite its deformed state.

One evening, when Polly and I were enjoying the warmth of the log fire, I noticed what I thought was a small mouse by the French windows. On closer inspection it was a different shape from our normal intruders. A shrew had decided to visit us. Now shrews rate highly on the 'nice animals chart', so it was allowed freedom of movement. For three or four days it sniffed its way around the edges of the room, not particularly bothered by our presence, yet at the same time keeping a respectful distance. It was a slow-moving, inquisitive creature but, when disturbed, it would hurry to some hiding place in another part of the lounge. When doing this, although not moving as swiftly as the mice we had encountered, its shape looked very mouse-like. This put doubts in my mind. Was this in fact a young mouse disguising itself as a shrew for the purpose of self-preservation?

A trap had to be laid, not only because of my uncertainty as to which species it was, but because a known mouse-hater was due to arrive in a week. If it were a shrew, could it be caught with the same bait as I used for mice? A search through Luke's encyclopaedia told me that shrews ate insects and spiders. The thought of fixing a dead spider to the mousetrap did not appeal. So cheese it had to be. In the morning the cheese had disappeared from the trap. It was a mouse then! The cunning little thing! On four consecutive nights this small mouse carefully lifted the cheese from the trap without setting it off. On the fifth night its previous soft touch was absent and it became ensnared. On removing the dead creature from the trap, I discovered it was in fact a shrew. It seemed I had made a discovery of extreme significance. In future encyclopaedias should read: the shrew . . . food – insects, spiders and Camembert cheese.

Rats were our biggest fear, though thankfully we never saw one. The only sign of rat-like activity came when we left a plastic football outside overnight. By the morning the ball was a flat, frayed piece of plastic. Our only explanation was that a rat had taken umbrage at such a gaudy object being left on its territory.

Catching mice (and shrews) was not the only art I managed to develop during our venture. My wood-chopping improved immensely. During winter, splitting wood with mallet and chisel became an everyday occurrence. My initial efforts were uninspiring. The chisel would sometimes become immovably embedded in the wood, or it would slice through it, landing with considerable force on my toes. My hands bore the scars of unco-ordinated and poorly aimed hammering. After a while, though, my action became more rhythmic, and I started to understand the wood. I knew what sort of wood split easily and how to deal with awkward knots. I felt as though I was mastering a difficult task, and so the job never became a chore.

Laying, lighting and maintaining log fires gained similar reward. I grew to realize that laying the fire too far back meant that much of the heat was lost up the chimney. I learned that a log fire needed to breathe, and ideally ashes six inches high should be left in the fireplace to give the new fire the best chance of success. I got to know how different woods were likely to react when burning. In autumn I created small fires with seldom more than a series of timid flames. By midwinter the fires encompassed the full fireplace. They had strength and character and would roar and spit with malice. Sometimes it was necessary to move the chair away from the fire to avoid the penetrating heat.

I am sure a country person would pour scorn on my woodcutting and firelighting ability, knowing other secrets of the wood that a lifetime in a rural community can give you. Even so, as we became more adept it seemed that we were successfully adjusting to the ways of the country. I felt that the wildlife, the people, and the countryside were starting to accept us. It was a good feeling.

8

A TOURIST'S EYE VIEW

On first arriving in Brittany, my tourist instincts led me to observe French people with interest, as they went about their everyday business. I was surprised to find that there were very few clues that told me they were French rather than British. It was no shock to discover a lack of the wide-striped jersey (it is more popular among the sailing fraternity of the Channel Islands) and Basque beret. The beret was sometimes worn, though the peaked cap was far more popular. The older women had a definite preference for wearing patterned dresses, often with scarves. Below pensionable age, the most surprising thing I noticed was that people tended to be less fashion-conscious, even scruffier than in Britain. The woman who shopped in dressing gown and slippers was an extreme example. Even so people generally took less pride in their appearance, especially at functions, where we usually felt overdressed. The renowned French elegance had not spread to rural France; it remained the domain of the Parisian.

Other visible French characteristics were the exaggerated use of arms, hands and face and the rubber-lipped distortions the mouth made to produce the wide variety of beautiful sounds used in the French language. Could the pouting of the lips, so important when speaking the language, have helped to give the French their amorous reputation?

There were certain individuals we passed, in and around Moncontour, who aroused our curiosity and at times inspired our imagination. One such person we would regularly see standing on the grass verge of a country lane about a kilometre from our house. We never saw him walking. He was always static until he heard our car coming. He would then slowly turn and stare at us as we approached. He watched us with a peculiar mixture of aggression and dreaminess. The car's mirror told us that his head had turned as we passed, as if he were a guard dog wary of an intruder.

Our first thoughts placed him as a tramp, whose home was a nearby ditch. This we soon discounted as from time to time he wore different clothing. We tried smiling at him and the occasional raised hand as we passed but we got no response, other than the familiar, vacant grimace. He started to make us feel uncomfortable. We had thoughts of him being involved in criminal activity, ranging from rape to bird's egg stealing.

Then one day he gave us the hugest smile, which displayed his few teeth and, more noticeably, a considerable number of gaps. We were no longer the strangers, the foreigners, the infidels. We had been accepted. By whom we did not know. Our imagination became more flippant. He just had to be the farmer's scarecrow. Then there was the punch-drunk boxer, with his former glory for all to see. Or was he the genuine village idiot, going about his daily work?

Another character was to be seen walking the streets of Moncontour and more particularly the main road skirting the town. He was short; rotund and wore thick glasses, which gave his eyes a bulbous quality. He would travel this road at the slowest of paces, and if there was no path, he would not use the grass verge or move to the side for a passing car. Doing this would destroy his methodical, walking rhythm. This at times became inconvenient for drivers, mainly because of the use of his walking stick. (The walking stick is used a great deal in France by the older generation. Much of the time it appears to symbolize seniority and wisdom, and suggests that the owner has had a tough existence, rather than him or her necessarily having extreme walking difficulties.)

His walking stick was gripped in his right hand, with his arm held straight out sideways. This had the effect of doubling his girth, resulting in him covering half of one side of the road. If a car came too close, he would turn and utter obscenities in the direction of the disappearing vehicle. It was as if he were guarding the old citadel by inspecting anyone who showed signs of being inhospitable. It was his decision as to their worthiness to enter the town. If a parked car or other obstruction made it difficult for traffic to pass him, he was undeterred and he would continue in the same ponderous, unflustered manner.

When talking with people, he gave the impression of being a dour personality.

Everybody though would have a word for him, even if it were only a shouted, '*Bonjour*!'

He was, as everyone seems to be in France, an accepted part of the community.

The lively community spirit to be found in Brittany stems from the strength of the family. Breton children's social life, especially in the country areas, is centred around the family. Even teenagers will rarely tread far from home. Carole, Emilie's sixteen-year-old sister, has mixed with adults all her life and is socially very mature. Despite this she has a naivety that would seldom be seen in a British teenager. Her outward display of enthusiasm about going to a *fête* or our arrival as visitors, would be more likely to receive a dismissive look from her British counterpart. She mixed with few people of her own age, so every glimpse of something out of the ordinary was treated as a special occasion.

Sophie, the daughter of the family I stayed with in Brest, was very similar. She was nineteen, was in her first year at medical school and owned her own car. She had every chance of using her home as merely a place to sleep, yet she was very much a part of the family unit. She, like Carole, possessed all the social graces of a mature adult, yet showed a child-like enthusiasm for certain television programmes. She would become totally involved in the plot of a film, sometimes needing to get her pillow to cuddle if the action became tense. She also showed admirable responsibility in the house, when Monique, her mother, was working. She was happy to take on the housewife role, despite the pressure of exams and a father who was at home all day with little to do.

Michel was a retired seaman, with a face strongly wrinkled by sun and salt. Since retiring he had become totally lethargic, occasionally pottering in the garden and going to bed early, where he could watch television uninterrupted. His only assistance in the house was to serve the wine, clean and open the oysters and sometimes to make and pour the coffee. These were manly things to do. In my experience, France is a fairly chauvinistic country, and Michel was a true disciple of the cause. So too were Monique and Sophie, for there were no signs of any haranguing or critical discontent. Indeed, rather than showing spiteful animosity, Monique talked to me of her concern for Michel's languid approach to life. She was a strong, fairly independent woman, yet family stability was all important to her.

Neighbourliness is almost a natural instinct in France. On first meeting the owner of the nearest house to La Ville Méen, he handed me a basket full of apples and pears. On the top lay two newly laid eggs.

When Kate, Luke and myself went for a short walk, an old woman, living in a nearby house, invited us in for a drink. At 10.30 in the morning I thought that a coffee would be just right, so I accepted the invitation. The children had some juice, but instead of coffee, a wine glass was placed in front of me, into which red wine was liberally poured. Early morning drinking had never been a feature of my routine and I wanted to decline, but the rich, red liquid was in front of me. So we drank and talked.

I saw the photographs of her family. Her husband had died ten years previously and her children had left home. She showed me around the house. It was massive for a woman on her own and in her early seventies. But it was the family home. She could not leave. One of her daughters would return to live there after she died. Despite its size, it was kept in immaculate condition. She was proud of her home. Saturday was the big day in her week, for her two daughters and grandchildren would dine with her. On Fridays we would see her slowly cycling into Moncontour to buy for this weekly feast. It seemed a lonely life, yet she obviously gained an enormous amount of pleasure from it.

That glass of red wine was my first experience of the apéritif. Normally I would be offered a gin, Pernod, Ricard or port. (Alcoholism is rife in France, though it is rarely wine that causes the problem.) If I called at someone's house, it was the standard practice to be asked in for an apéritif. The word, 'apéritif' has a tantalizing appeal when spoken in a French accent. I seldom declined. If I did the would-be host repeatedly insisted that I change my mind. Once enticed in, the drinks were poured, the 'nibbles' appeared and we would discuss the weather (such conversations are not the prerogative of the British), the children, Life.

These encounters would automatically begin and end with a statutory French greeting. With male friends it was always a handshake, a '*Salut*' and '*Ça va*'. No difficulty, you might imagine! It soon became evident, though, that I had to adjust the way I shook hands.

My public school upbringing had taught me that a firm handshake was a sign of true character and would improve my chances of getting a job when at an interview. In my late teens I attempted to annihilate whoever's hand I had to shake, in order to show them what a charismatic personality I was. Although I have now modified my grip, it still comes in the bone-crunching category. A Frenchman's handshake seems always to be of the limp-wristed variety. My first attempts received the sort of reaction that suggested my acquaintance had just received a momentary electric shock. The inappropriateness of my handshake was bluntly pointed out to me by one of my squash friends. He had been discomforted by my previous greetings and was obviously determined for revenge. He crushed my hand with preconceived intensity. No words were spoken. But his point was made. I had to start thinking of handshakes as being part of a friendly introduction rather than a power struggle.

Greeting women was never straightforward. Was it to be a handshake or a kiss? And if a kiss was it to be one, two or four? I would shake Madelaine's hand, kiss Emile once and Carole four times. I was perplexed. I asked my squash-playing friends (they were usually my means of unravelling mysteries). On this occasion they were of moderate help. They told me that it often depended on whichever part of France you were in, and that generally speaking, the greater number of kisses was an indication of a closer friendship. Apart from one kiss being normal when meeting a child, no specific definitions were forthcoming. It was obvious that people used deep-rooted intuition to determine a greeting. It would take a foreigner years to be able to react in the same way.

My uncertainty would often lead to a nervous beginning to a conversation.

Rather than considering what I was going to say, I would be thinking, 'How many times did she kiss me last time?' or 'She's quite old, it will probably be a handshake,' or 'What on earth shall I do? Oh I'll leave it up to her.'

I feel that part of the reason for the British being 'stand-offish' is because they will rarely initiate a French greeting. This is probably not because they don't want to, but because they are so bemused as to which one to choose.

Luke tried to sum up the difference between the French and British ways of greeting one another with a statement of ultimate simplicity.

'The French are very polite.'

I am sure he had thought of the throw-away comments of 'Morning!' and 'Hiya!' that he was used to hearing in Britain, and compared them with the formalities of the French. He, more than anyone, had appreciated this different approach. He positively basked in the warmth and feeling of security that emanates from the French way of saying 'Hello!'

* * *

My tourist's eye did not exclusively fall on the people of Brittany; it also often drifted towards the wide variety of buildings in the Breton towns. The medieval splendour of Moncontour and Dinan were overwhelming in their appeal: the towering walls and parapets, proud and assertive, yet hiding a bloody past; the narrow streets, enticingly unpredictable in their wandering steepness; the houses, each one with a marked individuality, whether sturdy and bold or leaning so precariously that you know a surveyor cannot possibly live within.

The buildings in the country were just as impressive. A house or farm could be found in every fold of the landscape. Each house (many, like ours, were converted barns) had a character of its own. They were untouched by the type of legislation which leads to architectural conformity. The one prerequisite seemed to be a dark grey, slate roof.

Some farms were magnificent. In many cases the owners had a basic way of life. A wood fire, the house's stout, thick, stone walls and its shutters (an unanswerable riposte to double-glazing salesmen) were thought sufficient to keep out the coldness of winter. There seemed to be a pride in being able to do without the gadgets and gimmicks of modern-day living.

The grandeur of some of these farmhouses belied the simplicity that lay within. To transport one to the Home

Counties would see it worth a massive sum, for some of these properties are of manorial proportions, large, rustically elegant and potentially majestic.

Alongside these fine buildings might well be a disused house or old barn in a state of disrepair. Indeed there are many such unattended buildings throughout Brittany. In Bréhand, a village nearby, it was on record that thirty-six houses were uninhabited. In Britain property is a precious commodity and empty houses would be snapped up for renovation within a sniff of them becoming vacant. France views property differently. Prices are fairly static, despite the ripples caused by 'greed-grabbing' German and British predators. Therefore the French see no gain in doing up a house which, in five years' time, will have only marginally increased in value.

The bargain that was to be had a few years ago is less easy to come by. Estate agents have kept in mind foreign markets to a certain extent when establishing house prices. Nowadays the bargain is to be found at root source, before the estate agent is involved. And this requires considerable inside knowledge.

9

SPORT BUT NOT COMPETITION

French people's involvement in leisure activities is as great as it is in Britain, yet in general they have not reached the same level of health consciousness as the British. The number of smokers of all ages is far greater than in Britain. Smoking is often seen in restaurants and not always at the end of a meal. Awareness of 'environmentally friendly' products is less acute in France. Hygiene and food packaging do not always emphasize the health merits of the product as much as the British equivalent. Also there are still a number of garages that do not sell lead-free petrol.

Although the heavy musk of sweat-laden French men and women is for the most part a memory of the past, the clinical concern for personal hygiene is not always evident after sporting activity. At the gymnastics class I attended most Thursday evenings, not one person sought a shower after the hour's session. The reason appeared not to be because I prepared for the activity in the same changing room, but because it was not felt to be an immediate necessity.

When I arrived on the first evening, the initial preamble took place in the women's changing room of Moncontour's sport's hall. One of my first questions was to ask where I changed (I was the only male in a group of ten).

The response was a dismissive wave of the hand, which I rightly took to mean, 'Don't worry, we all change in this room.'

I readily accepted the situation, musing that there was some sort of shift system in operation over use of the showers. At the end of the session everyone donned their tracksuits and made their way home, leaving me clutching my towel, soap, shampoo and smellies. I bathed at home.

In fact it is fair to say that this disinclination to shower is not necessarily an example of French people's disregard for personal hygiene. In many ways it is a comment on the different attitude people have to socializing in France. In Britain the sporting activity is nearly always a separate entity from social camaraderie. The British sportsperson is more likely to play the game, shower and then have a drink in a pub or clubhouse. In France the local sporting evening class tends to be a social event in itself; therefore there is no need for late evening debate. This is reinforced by the fact that activities tend to begin at a later time in France.

At my gymnastics class the first quarter of an hour invariably was a discussion as to who was not coming that week and why, together with some vital gossip. (Time was not lost, though, as the activity would continue after the expected finishing time.) In between exercises someone would halt proceedings by divulging another Moncontour scenario. For the ardent fitness fanatic it would have been frustrating.

When first deciding to join this evening class, I had assumed that *gymnastique mixte* did not involve jumping over boxes and horses but was the equivalent of British-style aerobics. Even so neither activity really appealed. (My previous sporting interests had always been dependent on a ball, whatever its shape or size.) So the incentive to participate lay in the opportunity to make French-speaking contacts, along with the fear in the back of my mind that the richness of French cuisine would make irreparable damage to my waistline.

I was a little disappointed to find that the activity revolved around stretching exercises. I had previously found satisfaction in huffing and panting my way around a squash court or rugby field. This more demure form of exercise was a little frustrating, particularly as I was the least capable member of the group. I blamed this on my inability to follow the instructions properly and the belief that women naturally had greater flexibility. I was less inclined to admit that my modest sporting achievements of the past had been gained through ungainly unorthodoxy rather than stylish technique and sylph-like manoeuvrability.

When I came home from my first session, I had a distinct lack of enthusiasm to return the following week. I was one of the youngest there, yet still one of the least able. I had understood very little of what was said, had been almost completely ignored, except by Sylvie, the gymnastics instructor, and felt physically unaffected by the activities.

In addition, Polly asked, 'How old were the people there?'

'Mostly middle-aged!' I retorted trying to gain her sympathy.

'About your age then,' was her spontaneous reply.

Like all great statements made by politicians, this was short, sharp and succinct. My attempt to be considered as a maturing young man was decimated in one curt, verbal blow. I had paid nothing, (this surely would never have been allowed in Britain) and I was fully prepared to wriggle away quietly, never to be involved again.

The next morning I awoke feeling muscle strain in many parts of my body. So it had done me some good! My wish to put myself in every possible French-speaking situation came to the fore and I was determined to go the following Thursday. I also decided to hand in a cheque to pay for a year's attendance before my resolve weakened.

For six or seven weeks I attended my evening class but I did not enjoy it. It became a begrudged duty. Sylvie was very supportive yet she failed to create the sort of involvement my more competitive instincts pined for. She was, in fact, part of the way through an instructor's course and was using the group to practise her newly learned ideas. This required her to refer perpetually to a sheet of exercises, which did not help continuity, as she would often stop demonstrating during a complicated manoeuvre in order to see what came next. The rustle of paper during wrist manipulation was one of my most vivid memories of the whole experience.

I found it difficult to communicate with the other members of the group. They were definitely wary of my presence. If we were asked to work in pairs there would be a rush to find a partner. The slowest moving person would work with me. This was made worse by the fact that the instructor, if she were needed to make up a pair, would give the order to work in twos and as she was speaking would grab one of her friends as her partner. Polly's assurance that in Britain men's attendance at aerobics classes was given similar treatment did not allay my feeling of isolation.

Matters were made worse by the deviousness of one of the participants. She was a sixty-two-year-old in marvellous physical condition, and had been working next to me on a stomach-strengthening exercise. During a lull in the music she let out an extremely loud fart. I knew it had come from her, so in noble, gentlemanly fashion I declined to look at her, for fear of causing her embarrassment. A few seconds later I casually looked up to find the whole class staring at me. This included the sixty-two-year-old, who had obviously chosen me as her fall guy. The women seemed even less inclined to work with me during the next two or three weeks. I felt even more isolated.

When one or two of my fellow participants started pretending to be rabbits, with limp-handed paws and twitching nose, (who said the only sense of humour the French have is imported?) I found it difficult to become part of the frivolity. It just didn't seem to have a place in evening class activity.

I was failing to accept that in France such recreation had a different role from in Britain. For most of the people these weekly sessions were their only genuine social contact outside their family environment. Also the demands of family life allowed little time for an activity that is followed by an hour of socializing. Therefore this mixture of exercise and discussion was a necessity, both strenuous and relaxing. It was an ideal situation for my language learning, yet I possessed an inbuilt conditioning which demanded more physical input.

It took a two week absence to put everything in perspective. Distancing myself from the group for a fortnight made me realize that I had been a little pompous with my expectations. The proceedings were pleasantly unpretentious and had to be taken for what they were. I was slowly getting to know the members of the group and was beginning to like a number of them. The sessions no longer became a chore. Although my knowledge of Moncontour gossip was minimal, I started to enjoy the laissez-faire attitude within the group, such as the mimicry of the photographer from the local newspaper. He had arrived smiling and full of bonhomie. He searched the room for the twenty or thirty people he was expecting to find. There were only four of us that week. Many plausible explanations were given. They did not suffice; his evening had been ruined. He left in a fit of pique.

Another light-hearted occasion was the time when Sylvie had to attend a *stage* on a Thursday in connection with her gymnastics course. She left a regular attender her valuable sheet of instructions, showing the exercises to be done. These instructions mostly consisted of stickmen in extremely uncomfortable positions. Teamwork was required to decipher the requirements. There was never any argument, but each person had to express a point of view. It took sometimes up to ten minutes to establish an exercise.

We would be asked to do the activity about ten times, but because discussion was even more prevalent than usual, counting was soon forgotten. Sometimes, because the conversation was so interesting, we might do the exercise about forty times. This did not mean extra exertion as, without Sylvie's prying eye, our stretching technique had been adapted so as to minimize the strain put on our limbs. We were schoolchildren trying to get away with as much as we could during the teacher's absence.

My experiences in the gymnastics class cannot be taken as the norm throughout France, though in general local authority-run courses do seem to have a similarly relaxed approach. Many activities will be taken very seriously, particularly when held at private clubs. The immense popularity of tennis has become particularly evident. It has far more television coverage than in Britain. Minor events will sometimes be televised. In addition the French tennis facilities are infinitely superior to those in Britain. The neighbouring village of Brehand possesses no more than ten shops, yet in its community sports hall it has an indoor tennis court. In Bristol there are no indoor tennis facilities. The fact that a small village like Brehand has a sports hall is not unusual. Local authorities are keen that there should be good sports facilities in their area. There are few small towns or large villages that do not have a sports complex of some sort.

The sport that foreigners particularly associate with France is *boules*. When I first enquired about it, I was puzzled by the response. There was talk of it sometimes being played indoors and of rolling it near to the *cochonnet* rather than throwing it. It was not until much later than I realized that the Breton game of *boules* was similar in style to bowls. The game I had thought was called *boules* was in fact *pétanque*. *Boules* are simply the balls that are thrown.

It is a game which seems so akin to the French character and embodies the pace of life in rural France. It is unhurried and accompanied by those meaningful gesticulations for which the French are so famous. A *pétanque* area entices all the faces of a previous age to one spot. As with my gymnastics class, it is a social event. Clusters of people will discuss the game and the event of the week with similar concern.

Interruptions of the game are severely frowned upon, as Keith, Annita and I found. We drove into what appeared to be a parking area. There were a few people standing near to their own cars, two of them carrying what looked like napkins. It seemed a peculiar place to have a picnic. It was not until these people started shouting in collective rage that we realized that something was amiss. Then Keith noticed a big, shiny, silver ball in the hands of one of the apparent picknickers. Suitably chastised, we looked to park elsewhere. As we drove away, I saw one of the *pétanque* players look at the damage our tyres had made to the playing area. I am sure that a totally different tactical approach was necessary for the game that afternoon.

Cycling is also recognized by foreigners as the sport of France. The number of cyclists on the roads suggests this is still the case. Professionally attired, the young and the old regularly travel the French roads. Other popular sports in France are football and basketball. Rugby is the domain of the south and volleyball and handball maintain strong support. One sport the French are truly smitten by is skiing. Its importance can be seen when looking at a school calendar. Half term in February lasts two weeks, presumably so parents have ample time to take their children skiing.

Even if a sport in France is taken seriously, it is still rare for *après sport* conviviality to take place, even in a club atmosphere. The few squash clubs in France can be considered unusual in this respect. It was through squash that I developed a number of sporting contacts. In Bristol the list of squash players better than me was interminably long. In France I found I was the best player within fifty miles of the nearest squash club. This is far less a comment on my ability than on the fact that most of the players have been playing squash for a short time. In addition very few people have been attracted to the sport.

This situation proved to be ideal for me. Had I been one of the worst players it would have been extremely difficult to arrange games. As it was a number of people were keen to play me. I got on particularly well with Michel, who not only wanted to play squash but also practise his English with me. There were many a raised eyebrow when people heard him speaking English and me French in the bar after a game. A bout of swiftly spoken, incomprehensible French with other players might be followed by Michel explaining what had been said, allowing me a stuttered contribution to the discussion.

Michel was a true example of a stereotyped Frenchman. He was a friendly, generous person but he was also a man of temperament. When watching him play squash it would have been easy to establish who had won the last point or was winning that particular game, even if you knew nothing about the sport. His use of eyes and mouth was that of a mime artist. Whatever his level of pleasure or discontent, it was displayed openly on his face. In addition, if he were really disgusted at the way he had played a rally, he would harshly chastise himself and, had he been on a tennis court, would surely have been warned for racket abuse. In the bar afterwards he would regularly comment on how he had played. This usually involved aggressive arm movements, necessitating those sitting nearest to him leaning back, away from his demonstration. These vigorous explanations were invariably accompanied by sound effects.

'*Claque, claque, claque!*' was one of his favourite expressions, used to describe hitting the ball hard.

He would also mimic the sound of a motor-bike revving, together with hand use of the throttle, to indicate involvement, determination, indeed anything which required adrenalin.

It was with Michel that I attempted my first joke in French. We were watching two beginners while waiting to go on court. One, concerned that he should have absolute protection from injury, was wearing skateboard-style elbow and knee pads; the other wore what looked like a kagoule.

I said to Michel, '*Un imperméable?*' holding my hand out, looking for drips of rain through the roof.

Michel burst out into raucous laughter. I was pleased. It was not until I had seen two or three more of these items of clothing that I realized they were in fact tracksuit tops. Perhaps Michel's laughter had not been in appreciation of my subtle sense of humour after all.

After I had played at the club for seven or eight weeks, I learned that the club team had gained an anonymous sponsor.

I was pleased because this must mean we would have games against other teams. At last competition! My assumption was false, as no games were arranged. I was puzzled. Sponsorship was surely to do with advertising, so why would a sponsor want to hide his or her identity? In actuality the money was to go towards paying for the squash courts on Friday evening in order that there should be team practice. In some way the sponsorship also infiltrated into drinking time. I was a little confused, yet far from dissatisfied. Towards the end of our stay, it was revealed that our generous benefactor was the father of one of the younger players.

I gained a good deal more from these Friday sessions than simply cheap squash. They gave me an insight into French culture and regular contact with the language, but I was also able to develop one or two lasting friendships.

In addition my playing at the club enabled me to hold a squash-playing licence, essential for entry into the numerous tournaments held in France. The tournament that had caught my eye was the Brittany Veteran's Championship to be held in Brest. I had recently reached the qualifying age of forty-five and thought that, for the first time ever, I had a chance of winning a tournament. Most of the best French squash players were young. Surely those over forty-five would not have played the game as long as I had. This could be my opportunity! I would have to return early from our winter half term trip to Britain and would have no car, yet the possibility of my first ever cup was incentive enough. My enthusiasm to succeed was emphasized by the fact that I took to running in an attempt to prepare myself. Such dedication had never been contemplated before.

I arrived in Roscoff on the overnight ferry, to find that the train service would fail to get me to Brest in time for the expected start of the tournament. My resolve did not weaken, so I experienced the foolhardy recklessness of a French taxi driver keen to return to Roscoff as soon as possible. He dropped me in Morlaix where I caught a train which would ensure I was not late.

At the squash club I eagerly scoured the draw, only to find my name was not there. I sought the championship organizer, who explained that he had read the small print of the regulations and had found that it was necessary to be resident for two years before entering a provincial tournament. My weekend looked to be a miserable affair. He sensed my disappointment and suggested that, if I were interested, he would find a couple of players for me to play. He also offered his house for me to stay the night. I accepted his invitation and thoroughly enjoyed the weekend.

One thing that the weekend brought home to me was how trusting the French are. My host wanted to get an early night and did not wish to join the late-night revelry of some of the other players. Rather than insist I go with him, he suggested that I could come home when I wished. I expected him to hand me a key; after all he lived in the heart of the city. Instead he said he would leave the garage and back door open. When I returned in the early hours I found his use of the word 'open' was literal. Both doors were invitingly ajar. To do such a thing in a British city would be unthinkable.

When buying drinks in a French bar, that same trust is in evidence. It is the custom not to pay for drinks when you order them. The tendency is to pay for them on leaving. In Brest I even had to remind the barman that I had not paid for a round of drinks ordered the previous evening. The amount owed is rarely written down and can often lead to complications at the end of an evening at the bar. Such difficulties are unimportant and often lead to someone paying more than he or she should. In France to be generous is far more important than the need to spend exactly the same amount as your drinking partner.

Throughout Brittany there appears not to be that need for elaborate security. The locking of cars is more open to whim than necessity. And I don't remember seeing one burglar alarm while in France. (The vicious dog and shutters are often felt adequate.) Also the French seldom ask to see a credit card when accepting a cheque, and if 'plastic' is required, the signature is rarely compared.

Why should the relative nirvana of affluent America produce a frightened society, obsessed with security? Do they breed fewer people with criminal inclinations in France? Or it is the strength of the family which has kept most people on the chosen path? After all, in Paris, where criminal activity is more frequent, the family is far more segmented than in the rest of the country.

The family certainly plays a strong part in developing the

sporting interests of the young. Most children will be encouraged, indeed expected, to participate in at least one sport. They respond to this family stimulation and having gained a fair degree of competence, usually maintain their sporting interest in adulthood.

In some ways parents' and teachers' sporting expectations are greater in France than Britain. On sports day in Britain, junior school children are usually asked to run one hundred metres. The less gifted may often choose to participate in a three-legged or egg-and-spoon race. Before Moncontour School's sports day, Kate informed me that the children were expected to run further than in her previous primary school. I was a little concerned that her small nine-year-old body would be pushed to the limit in a race of anything up to two hundred metres.

Sports day did not simply involve children from Moncontour. Five other schools were invited to a running track in the stadium of the nearby village of Quessoy. Parents were asked to assist in transporting the children, so I volunteered my services, happy to watch my children's participation in a French sports day, even though I was the only Moncontour parent to stay and watch the proceedings.

The first race was for the five or six-year-old girls. They were lined up, given their starting orders and set off at no more than a jog. I was surprised. There was no aggressive running, no attempt to win the race. Not even as they approached the finishing line was there any discernible quickening of pace and as the leading girl passed the line there was no sign of elation. She just kept on running. So did the rest of the children. How commendable! A genuine warm-up lap before the real racing began! Even so it did seem a bit far for them to run in order to avoid strains. This assumption proved false for, instead of stopping with the starter, having run one lap, they proceeded to continue round the track.

I pushed my way through to the information board. These tiny individuals were being asked to run a thousand metres. Further consultation led to the discovery that the boys of CE1, Luke's class, had to cover 1250 metres and the girls of CM1, Kate's class, were expected to run 1500 metres. I also noticed that boys were not only separated from the girls in these races but were expected to run further than the girls in the same class.

I was shocked. I believed that half the children simply would not finish. Again I was wrong. The fat, the frail, the unco-ordinated all finished. Each individual seemed to get exhausted enjoyment from completing the race, however slowly. This satisfaction was reinforced by them being given many vocal congratulations and pats on the back by others from the same school.

This support and togetherness was good to see. But another aspect of the event, which was both refreshing and unexpected, was the lack of competitiveness which permeated the proceedings. I had heard much talk about British schools trying to subdue some of the more competitive urges in children. Despite this I had watched races on sports day and listened to the first, second and third being hailed victorious over a loudspeaker.

On this French sports day much emphasis had been placed on the unimportance of victory. In two or three of the races, a child had shot out in front on the first lap. One of the teachers rushed onto the track and encapsulated the individual in his arms. The athlete was given a stern lecture about racing on his or her own, before being allowed to continue with the following group of runners. I was to find that a non-competitive approach had been stressed before arriving at the stadium too. When I saw the distance Kate had to run, I found her, to give her some advice as to how to achieve victory. She quickly interrupted my words of tactical wisdom, by telling me that she had been asked to run with somebody else and not to try and win the race. And so it was! Whenever possible, children ran together, and there was no specific acclaim for the runner who crossed the finishing line first. Every child knew that he or she had achieved something.

Moncontour School's close affinity with the other small primary schools in the area was again emphasized when a day's cycle ride was organized for the older children. As with the sports day, it was to be no easy option. The course involved visiting all six schools, thirty-eight kilometres in all. Cars were needed for general safety and to pick up any cyclists or bicycles that might collapse under the strain. After some persuasive pleas from Kate, I agreed to follow the Moncontour contingent, though without any natural enthusiasm.

It proved to be a tremendous day. The children, free of the normal school drudgery and knowing that to complete the course was a worthwhile achievement, enjoyed every tiring moment of it. All, that is, but one! His bike had fallen apart after half a kilometre. He spent the rest of the day in the back of a parent's car, with a stern face, unimpressed by the proceedings.

Each school was a resting station and provided cakes, biscuits and drink to revive any flagging hearts. Three of the schools considered the less active helpers by supplying alcoholic refreshment. Kir at one, beer at another and red wine at the next did wonders for our morale, though the powers that be might not have been impressed in the event of an accident. As it was, there were no disasters and a satisfying day was had by all.

It struck me that there would be no bitter, inter-village rivalry, when these children reached secondary school. The primary school teachers will have minimized the possibility of such attitudes at an early age. Much 'clan' hostility stems from the insecurity of not knowing what the other group is like. These children have experienced each other's environments and have participated together in a truly non-competitive activity. They are no longer total strangers to one another.

I would imagine that France will continue to produce few world champions. At any rate not until its schools stop having an all-embracing approach to sport, and its children become more single-mindedly obsessed by the need to win.

10

TRAINING AND TRAINS

Our house in France was embedded in the heart of rural Brittany, mingling with the farms and smallholdings that were once the embryo of the French economy. Indeed agriculture is still immensely important to France. If someone is an *agriculteur* he is taxed at an extremely low rate. It is rumoured that people holding down regular jobs will rear twenty chickens in the back gardens, so allowing them to put *agriculteur* on their tax forms.

Such incentives have not led to complacency, resulting in the farmers sticking to rigid, traditional ways. The picture of an old, Breton farmer, using donkey and plough and still milking by hand, is all but a myth. Only the occasional owner of a smallholding will resort to primitive methods. The vast majority of *agriculteurs*, however small their enterprise, will use modern techniques and machinery to establish their livelihood. It is most likely they will be able to do this, as a result of belonging to one of the co-operatives which first sprung up after the Artichoke War in the 1960s.

Until the early 1960s the dealers were in control of setting the price of produce. The proud, tight-lipped independence of the older farmers ensured that the dealers could haggle for a low price. In 1960 a group of younger growers decided to challenge the situation when the price of artichokes collapsed. They drove lorries full of artichokes to Paris and sold them on the streets. In the following year the price of all vegetables became ridiculously low, so the growers responded with the most aggressive form of peaceful demonstration they could muster. They dumped lorry-loads of potatoes and artichokes in the streets of certain towns, preventing the movement of traffic. The historically rebellious nature of the Bretons was still in evidence, even in times of peace.

These demonstrations prefaced the establishment of co-operatives, which helped individuals, maintained standards and in some cases led to agricultural, market research. This new-found, professional approach ensured that the Breton farmers' considerable reputation remained intact. Even so discontent is often close at hand and they, along with the rest of the French farming population are sceptical of the Common Agricultural Policy in the single European Market. The need for extensive investment to maintain technological competitiveness with neighbouring countries is of paramount importance. The pressure of monetary policies, variable quality of produce and the lack of standardized pay for farm workers are also contentious uncertainties. In spite of this, the tenacious instincts of the Breton should ensure that the agricultural industry in Brittany endures well into the twenty-first century.

It is not just in agriculture that the Bretons, indeed the French, possess a professional outlook. They have a strong work ethic. This is best displayed by their attitude to training. Firms spend a substantial amount of money on training in the expectation of gaining true expertise.

The importance placed on learning practical skills can be seen in the government's insistence that no one is fully qualified until he or she has done ten years' training. Most trades and professions follow this edict, though the idea has not yet been fully implemented. Our postman had seven years of training, which included a year of work experience in Paris. In Britain it is a matter of weeks before you plod the streets as a fully fledged postman.

Examples of the well-trained worker can be seen everywhere. When staying in a Carnac hotel, I was impressed by the competence of a waitress who looked closer to sixteen than twenty-one. She had an understanding of wine, could carry two plates in one hand with elegance and a lack of fuss and possessed a quiet confidence beyond her years. The quality of her training was there for all to see.

Perhaps the best example of professional pride can be seen when looking in virtually every French shop window. An attractive display on the counter or in the window is the norm in France. Presentation is part of the shopkeeper's art, similar to the ability to prepare meat or bake bread.

The two experts who tended our spluttering central heating system showed pride in their work in contrasting ways. The first engineer we called out was quick to apply himself to the task. Experience or a sixth sense led him to the boiler room without my directions. Chopped wood I had stored there was speedily ejected, to allow him sufficient working space. I was confident we had the right man for the job.

After about twenty minutes I was keen to know how the work was progressing. I enquired of Polly whether it was customary in France to make workmen cups of coffee. She did not think so but thought it might be prudent to ask all the same. His response to my question was a look of incredulity. This was supported by the comment that he would have a drink when he had finished. It was obvious that the job had to be done satisfactorily before liquid refreshment could even be considered.

About ten minutes after I had returned to the house, I noticed him making his way to his van. I assumed he was getting a necessary tool and was surprised to see the van disappear up the drive. Perhaps he had gone back to base for a spare part. He could not have finished; he had not claimed his coffee. Then I considered the way he had walked to the van. A picture of Fagin immediately came to mind. He took short, shuffling steps, almost as if he were on tiptoe. In one hand he clutched a collection of tools, but the other hand hung limply from his arm, as if in the set position to pick pockets. His hunched shoulders surely suggested he was concealing something. His gaunt face with a bony protruding nose completed his criminal image. My inner-city paranoia proved to be ill-founded, for on entering the boiler room I found that the central heating was working again, and not even my precious mallet and chisel had been touched.

I was puzzled by him not coming in for a coffee and explaining what he'd done, though the disappointment was greater when the heating broke down in the middle of a very cold evening.

Polly telephoned his number the next day and left a message with his wife. The following afternoon we heard his van coming to a halt on the gravel. We waited for his knock but it was not forthcoming. He had gone straight to the boiler room again. I followed him in there and started explaining what had happened, only to be stopped mid-sentence by his outstretched hand, boldly raised like a traffic policeman's. This was reinforced by some undecipherable comments which, as they were spoken in a confident manner, I took to mean that he had everything under control. Again I left him to it and again I saw him scurrying for the van.

I quickly went outside wanting to say, 'Please would you come in and explain the present state of play.'

Unfortunately I not only had to transfer my thoughts into French but also decide what tone of voice to use, in order not to sound rude. While pondering such complexities he had disappeared.

The problem still persisted and we spent another evening draped in thick jumpers and clustered around the log fire. Polly's phone call the following day again found the engineer's wife at home. This time she became embroiled with our difficulties. She showed genuine concern that young children had been living in freezing conditions and she promised, most forthrightly, to send him to us as soon as he came in. In less than an hour a rather disgruntled engineer again started work on the boiler. We were determined he should not escape this time. I manned the window, ready to shout to Polly as soon as he appeared from round the side of the house. She was then to rush out to prevent his departure. The plan worked, though Polly received only a mumbled hope that he had cured the trouble. This hope did not materialize and we decided to try another firm.

For the sake of the owners we felt honour-bound to query the bill when it arrived. Polly was concerned about this, as she knew very well that to argue on the telephone is one of the most difficult skills to master in a foreign language and she was not looking forward to the ordeal. She need not have worried for the bill never came. Was it because the engineer was so far behind with his paperwork that he had not got round to sending it? Or was it because, in being unable to correct the fault, his pride had been severely dented? If so how could he send us a bill?

The engineer from a different firm also encountered difficulties, having to visit us four times before identifying and rectifying the problem. On each visit he offered profuse apologies for his apparent inadequacies. It soon became obvious that the job had become a personal challenge to him. He left his home phone number, which we were to contact at any time in an emergency. When we went away for a few days, he volunteered to pop in every day to check whether it was still working. Such commitment made me think he might be the owner of the central heating firm. In fact he was simply one of the engineers.

When he had finally diagnosed the fault and fitted the new part, he joined us for a cup of coffee. In his previous conversations he had been reticent to talk of his work. His brow had been creased through serious contemplation. He had seemed sullen. Now that he had succeeded in mending the system, his face relaxed and he talked ardently, displaying all his peacock feathers. He had described everything he had done in the four visits, as precisely as if it were a surgical operation. His arms and hands intimated any degree of difficulty involved, with sometimes dramatic effect.

Next came a few of his success stories in other houses in the neighbourhood. Now that he had completed his task, he was keen to dispel any doubts we might have as to his ability. His enthusiasm was refreshing, especially seeing the satisfaction he gained from completing a good job. I felt certain the story of our system would be included in his repertoire of central heating tales.

We thought we might need another professional after our February half-term break in England. Our fear arose from a conversation with a neighbouring smallholder on the day we were due to return to Britain. The weather was the farmer's unquenchable hobby. When passing he always wanted to stop for a three minute discussion and the first and most detailed topic was always the weather. This occasion proved no exception.

'It's cold!'

My every movement conveyed my agreement.

'There will be snow by the end of the week.'

'We will miss it. We are going to England today.'

The look of shocked concern on his face was a shock in itself. Usually he maintained the same serious expression whatever the situation. Normally his head seemed to nestle in his massive neck rather than on it and was unable to turn without the rest of his body. When he spoke only his lips visibly responded. All other movement of the jaw was lost in the secret folds of his taurine neck. On this occasion both face and neck reacted to my innocent remark.

There followed an intense lecture on what to do to prevent frozen pipes. I nodded or muttered knowingly to his instructions. In truth I only half-understood his suggestions, the extent of my plumbing vocabulary being rather limited. The tone of his voice became more severe, indicating that his advice was to reach a crescendo of importance.

'And the toilet?'

'No problem!'

My complacency needed to be destroyed. This was done by means of a dialogue of technical complexity, most of which was beyond my comprehension. When talking, our neighbour's arms would usually remain static at his side. They did not hang straight but were permanently bent at the elbow in manly pose. The need to assist his detailed oration brought them out of muscle-bound inactivity. Their primary use was to create the shape of a u-bend waste-pipe. There are three different types of waste-pipe in France and each one required contorted, visual effects, in addition to a verbal description. After a while it became apparent that there is one type of piping which causes problems in cold weather. The effect of the damage that could be caused by sub-zero temperatures was amply demonstrated by him opening his arms and extending his stubby fingers. This was accompanied by a puffing of the cheeks and the sound of a loud explosion. The pipe and presumably its contents would be splattered to all parts of the room. I was not to worry though. The remedy was to pour *antigel* generously into the toilet. I thought that *antigel* was some sort of disinfectant. It was, according to my well-thumbed dictionary, anti-freeze. We had none and there was little time left before we had to leave in order to catch the ferry. So the water in the toilet remained 'neat'.

On next meeting our neighbour, I was happy to be able to recount the lack of an exploding u-bend. The excitement aroused by our previous meeting had disappeared.

Instead I received a poker-faced 'You were lucky!' and one almost begrudged compliment on the durability of our toilet.

Another sign of a good professional approach was evident when dealing with France Telecom. During the first week we were in Brittany, Polly went to their offices in St Brieuc to ask for a telephone line to be installed at our house. Response to our needs was quick and within a week we were in contact with the outside world. The French telephone system is said to be one of the most technologically advanced in the world and one of their most notable achievements is the widespread use of Minitel. When at the France Telecom offices she was given a lucid account of the benefits of Minitel by an astute assistant showing good saleswoman technique.

Minitel is a computerized machine that is connected to the telephone. It can be found in large post offices as well as homes. It can be a telephone directory, a weather forecaster, a ferry crossing information provider; its list of uses is endless. It can even give the answers to the *baccalauréat* exam, the day after it has been taken. What was most appealing, though, was that the basic set was available to any telephone user free of charge. To be offered this machine for nothing was too much of a temptation. We had to have one.

From time to time it was a very useful piece of equipment, but to begin with it became a plaything. Polly tried a psychometric test of intelligence. The result was very pleasing. Then the cost of the test came up on the screen – eighty francs. This was not so pleasing. I certainly realized the reason for our Minitel being presented to us free of charge.

Despite there being technological magnificence in some areas, in others France is behind the times. For instance in interviews or chat shows each person will invariably have an individual, hand-held microphone. Also there is an unco-ordinated plethora of wires that move from house to house at roof-top level. It is as if the French are trying to maintain these lines because they are a part of a town's charm, rather than collecting and encasing them to make them less unsightly.

Like the telephone system, French trains are something very special. Not only does travelling on them make you feel a part of the French way of life, but they normally run according to schedule. I'll repeat that: French trains run on time. We were amazed to find that our first six trips by train brought us to our destination exactly at the expected time. Our seventh excursion arrived a mere two minutes late. Shortly before we pulled into the station, profuse apologies were forwarded to us over the intercom for the delay.

The one exception to this rule was the time when Polly was travelling back from Paris on a TGV (*train à grande vitesse*), faster, cleaner and more comfortable than the British 125. It broke down and rolled to a halt, annoyingly only a few kilometres from where we lived. Everyone had to get out and wait for the next train.

The change in the travellers was immense. Prior to the breakdown there was a studious, serious atmosphere. Virtually no words were spoken. Everybody was ensconced in a book or newspaper. Nobody appeared to have unwound from what was obviously a working day in Paris. To read in a concentrated fashion almost seemed like an expected extension of their working lives. For many the only sign of relaxation was the occasional sip of mineral water from a plastic cup. The one exception to this was a man who regularly filled his cup with red wine. Closer inspection of the book he was reading suggested that he was in fact an Englishman.

When everybody had heaved themselves out of the carriages, a dramatic transformation was immediate. Rather than there being a few grumbles and groans, everyone (except those of British descent) started speaking in a high-pitched, energetic, almost feverish manner. Highly abusive condemnation of the rail system ranged from refusing to travel on a TGV ever again, to a character assassination of the minister in charge of the railways. The straight, serene faces had disappeared; instead were venomous, fiery-eyed, arm-flinging individuals. These individuals gradually formed quite large groups embroiled in fervent discussion.

Soon what appeared to be a train, travelling in the right direction, became visible in the distance. The hoped-for train was in fact an engine. As it passed, a man shouted an enquiry as to how it was to accommodate all the people on the platform. This lightened the atmosphere a little. Everyone was still outward-going and opinionated, yet people's comments were far more flippant than cutting.

The next train struggled through the station, laden with new cars. The same wag as before remarked that the authorities had been so good as to deliver their own cars to those waiting, in order to minimize any inconvenience. Further light-heartedness followed until impatience and exasperation took over.

After about an hour everybody crammed themselves onto

the next train. More consternation occurred, for it seemed that many of these TGV travellers had not had the indignity of standing on a train before. Booking a seat in advance on a TGV is compulsory.

The guard was keen to point out over the intercom that compensation was readily available because of the delay. Polly eventually received seventy francs recompense.

The TGV service has occasionally been affected by French people's often indignant concern for their rights. One of the favourite targets of a *manifestation* is for the protesters to sit on the railway track in front of a train. A delayed TGV is sure to make headline news. Paris is the obvious place to hold *manifs*, whether on a railway line or elsewhere, and the Parisians almost expect them as a part of city life.

During a lecture that Polly was attending in Paris, much commotion and stamping of feet was heard below the lecture theatre. The lecturer's immediate response to the noise was that it must be a *manif*. This prematurely curtailed the lecture, as the students sought a good view from the window to watch the proceedings. There was no sign of anyone, even though the noise still continued. It transpired that it was simply a drama class, taking place directly below the lecture theatre.

The French have a strong sense of right and wrong and are seldom frightened of voicing their opinions. Indeed they need time to stress fully their points of view. A midday meal followed by the children giving an exhibition of country dancing was arranged to raise money for school funds. Parents were invited to school at half past eleven for an aperitif. The dancing was due to begin at three o'clock, but it was unable to take place at the designated time. Conversation was so intense that the half past twelve meal did not finish until just before four o'clock. So the nervous dancers had to wait until Moncontour and the state of the world have been discussed in full before they could perform. Such cultural activity had to take second place to more urgent matters of the moment.

A move towards yellow-lighted legality

The jaws of no return

Cast from the past

Publicité

Vive la difference!

The tourist information centre in Lamballe

The important gossip of the day

Pondering the past

The lack of building symmetry in Dinan

Splendidly antiquated, yet in need of its terraced support

Craftsman at work

Display is everything

Madame and her wares

You know the bread is fresh, when you can still hear it sizzling

Creative use of scourer to prepare the mussels

Après-dinner depression

St Mathurin's image with frontal bone embedded in forehead

A relaxing view of the port in Dinan

The Pardon of St Mathurin as depicted in
Moncontour's Catholic church

Medieval Dinan

A discerning eye

The roads are paved with creativity

Crêpes – before

And after (nearly)

House with enormous potential! A must for the innovative purchaser!

Beauty and the beast of a problem

Vive la France!

11

A HOLIDAY WITHIN A HOLIDAY

To go on holiday when already on holiday may be considered excessive. Even so, during our stay we decided to go cruising on the French canals. Like moving to France, this idea could be categorized as an adventure. The family's collective swimming ability was unimpressive (Luke in fact could not swim). Also our knowledge of propelling anything larger than a canoe was nil. Despite this everyone liked the idea, and one sunny morning in May we set off for Messac to sally forth on a cruiser for a week.

My first, tentative, carefully placed step on board had all the marks of a true landlubber. I gripped the side of the cabin with one hand and with the other clutched Luke's hand with vice-like protection. I did not relax until we were well ensconced inside the cabin. Happily we were not simply flung an instruction book and wished bon voyage. An engineer came on board with us and told us how everything worked in very good English. He then volunteered to accompany us through the first lock, a mere two kilometres away. He steered the cruiser out of the small marina and then in mid-channel offered me the controls. It all seemed quite easy. Despite our snake-like approach to the lock, I felt it would not take me long to master the fault of over-correction. Confidence didn't ooze, but it did trickle.

Forty metres from the lock the engineer told me to slow down and give one blast on the horn as a warning to the lock-keeper. My reflex response to orders has never been so sharp. This occasion was no exception. My hesitance was diagnosed as incompetence and the engineer dealt with the operation. To an observer he had given me responsibility for the process of manoeuvring through the lock. In actuality his hand was but a fraction away from the gear stick and steering wheel, adjusting whenever I veered from the chosen path. The only time I felt in control of the boat was as it was coming out of the lock. This proved that his initial assumption was justified, for I started to steer the cruiser straight for the stone-slabbed jetty. The now more ruffled engineer prevented the impending crash and then most skilfully brought the boat to the side, this time without any mock assistance from me. He swiftly departed, leaving my confidence shattered.

We had intended to go north and moor for the night a few kilometres upstream. This would have meant turning round and immediately going back through the lock. An alternative plan was necessary. So we faint-heartedly decided to moor where we were for the night, after cruising for half an hour or so on our side of the lock. I spent much time that night reading all the relevant literature as preparation for the following day. The signal I came across, which stuck in the mind the most, was the one which required four long blasts on the horn, meaning, 'my boat is out of control'.

The next day, despite a certain amount of trepidation, we passed through the first lock very smoothly. The lock-keeper required no assistance, as our guide to cruising suggested, because she manipulated the locks by remote control. This was pleasing, because at this stage of our holiday, to step from boat onto metal ladder with a turbulent swell below, did not appeal.

Remarkably few problems were caused by going through the locks. The method of Polly standing at the front of the boat, making sure my aim was true, and me at the helm proved successful. It very nearly failed us, though, towards the end of the holiday. The lock in question was in a very picturesque spot, near a water-mill. It had attracted a large number of families partaking in the traditional French habit of going for a Sunday afternoon walk. On seeing our cruiser approach, about sixty people clustered round the edges of the lock, like ants to a blob of honey. They had been waiting all afternoon for a boat to pass through and were keen to watch a true boatman manoeuvring his craft. The relaxed use of the wheel that I had gradually developed was soon lost. I felt like the entertainer, or sportsman, who freezes on the big occasion.

'More to the left.'

'Right.'

'Right!'

'Left again!'

Polly's voice was becoming higher and sounding more concerned with each instruction. The noise of excited discussion emanating from the crowd suggested disaster. But in spite of our uncertain approach, we managed to squeeze in the lock without touching the sides. This success had not fooled our audience, judging by their muffled expressions of surprise. I had been unable to conceal my novice's tag and was thankful for the uncritical peace to be found round the next bend.

Although passing through locks caused me no difficulty, having to stop before a lock opened did prove a problem. In order to stop the cruiser it was necessary to put the engine in reverse. Unfortunately the steering wheel became redundant when in reverse. In my inexperienced hands it often led to our boat straddling the canal and, facing the bank, gently drifting sideways towards the lock. Much heavy-handed use of the gear stick, first forward, then reverse, was my only answer to right the situation. Had I been driving a car it would surely have suffered from a burnt-out clutch. Often after a few minutes I would submit and cower in the comparative safety of the reeds.

Such difficulties were minute compared with my biggest faux pas, that of misinterpreting a danger sign placed importantly in the middle of the canal. For some reason I thought it meant, 'there is danger if you keep this sign to your left', instead of its true meaning, 'danger if you go to the left'. I was soon to find what the danger was, as a raucous, grating noise from the bottom of the cruiser interrupted the day's tranquillity. This coincided with the boat slowing down and the engine sounding extremely tired. I put the engine in reverse. There was no movement. What were we to do? Polly commented that it was a good thing we had a bike on board, because I could cycle and get help. I had to point out that I could neither ride nor walk on water. The thought of a rock sticking up into one of the rooms below sprang to my mind. Further inspection found this not to be so – yet.

Another minute of dithering followed. Then, trusting that our life-jackets were in good working order, I chose to be bold. Full throttle forwards! The cruiser ground its way along the rocks very slowly. The noises from beneath were varied and ugly. The engine struggled to sound convincing, yet it whirred on and on, until it forced the cruiser off the ledge of rock and into the open channel. Polly rushed into the cabin for any sign of water. None was visible. We continued on our way as if nothing had happened. The incident wasn't mentioned again, until the children were asleep. By that time we could joke about our being on the precipice of a disaster.

I wondered whether Polly and I would have reacted as calmly as we did had we been without the children. I think there would have been much more of a show of exasperation and annoyance. There could even have been a different outcome. With Kate and Luke on board, our approach was geared towards ensuring that they did not feel frightened. Our level-headed attitude was an innate response to protect those very close to us. Signs of emotion and fear could have led them to panic, the sort of reaction which could have endangered their lives.

In spite of my steering idiosyncrasies, our week afloat was a tremendous experience. In our French house we had encountered the type of peacefulness enjoyed by someone recuperating in a country nursing home. The same quality was present on the cruiser, though it seemed to be enhanced by our gentle progress through the countryside. To someone in a stressful job, the contrast would be positively therapeutic. The lilt of the boat and the opportunity to observe and appreciate the countryside in slow motion had an almost hypnotically relaxing effect. A car drive to the country would be no comparison.

Many memories have survived. There was the occasional small village or hamlet with its unpretentious, rustic charm. It often possessed a small dimly lit general store or bar, whose users would give visitors cold stares, suggesting that trespassing was a heinous crime. There was the dog sniffing in puzzled disbelief, for it had not realized that the water vole it had disturbed had made its v-shaped escape across the canal. The weirs and their shining symmetry had an almost magnetic fascination for me. So did the birds. I particularly enjoyed watching the climbing nuthatch and grey heron. At first the heron was ankle deep in water and totally still in expectation of a fishy delight; next, disturbed by our arrival, it would slowly open its enormous wings and, like a billowing sheet, alternately flap and glide its way to another favourite haunt. A special sighting, though, was the small flash of red which darted past our boat. A canal holiday surely needs a kingfisher for total aesthetic satisfaction.

A less attractive memory was the sight of the roots of trees close to the canal's edge. They had been infiltrated by the wash of the boats, moving too quickly along the canal. Some had succumbed to the water's nagging jaws and had been felled, leaving their massive roots as a bulwark to further bank erosion. Others relied on the thickest, staunchest part of their roots to remain aloft, though time was not with them. Nature, on the other hand, had made use of their plight, for moorhens and ducks occasionally used the water beneath these foundations as play areas for their young.

Perhaps the most memorable feature of the trip was the variation of light and shade. Most of the previously mentioned were fleeting images, yet the effects created by sun and moon were with us throughout the journey. Sometimes individual rays of light could be seen squeezing their way through dark foliage. You could follow the slanting beam until it hit the water. There it left its glare, to make anyone undignified enough to stare too long, feel uncomfortable. The shadows made by the trees and bushes were a creative delight to the children. At their blackest they made the canal appear dramatic, which belied its normal, flat, subdued nature. At other times the shadows gave the water a variety of shades, which transformed the canal's potential greyness into an abundance of subtle hues, the envy of any Impressionist painter. Even the rounded symmetry of a bridge's reflection in the water accentuated its beauty.

It is not surprising that the romantic writer falls in love with moonlight on water, for it possesses a soft mystique. It is also more perceptive than the sun's rays. The sun may be able to seek out many a hidden cranny that the moon will never find. However the moon is able to highlight the gentlest of ripples, that the sun's ferocity neglects. Light and shade, reflection and shadow meld together to create a soothing serenity.

The almost complete lack of cars and people also enhanced this feeling of peace. At first it seemed strange yet at the same time refreshing. The sight of any mechanical device from the twentieth century was an intrusion on privacy, whether it be a distant factory or merely a car. The only marvel of modern machinery which did not annoy was our own cruiser. But that did not count!

Groups of people made me feel uncomfortable when watching us, as their awe-struck gaze suggested we were zoo curiosities. Occasional walkers and fishermen seemed a natural part of the scene, though, but not all the fishermen reciprocated those sentiments. Towards the end of the holiday we created a game to determine fishermen's reactions to a cheery wave. Three categories were devised. The first was the friendly smile and vigorous wave. The second was the half-smile and minimum of hand acknowledgement, restricted so as not to be discernible to nearby fishermen. Lastly there was the eagle-eyed stare at the float. This suggested that the fisherman was concentrating so intensely that he had not even noticed our presence. It did seem, though, that it was a greater indication as to his philosophy on pleasure crafts' use of canals. Clue to success in the game often depended on how active the fisherman was before we reached his float. The more energetic he was the more chance there was of him cheerfully accepting our right to travel the canal. Happily the first category was the most common.

Apart from the lock near the water-mill, the greatest number of people we encountered was at Bourg des Comptes. On first approaching this largish village we noticed a group of canoeists playing some form of water polo. I sent out a blast on the horn, expecting them to scatter to either bank. I slowly steered the boat closer to the activity and again used the horn. Still no reaction! We edged nearer, but still the game continued. I felt that my booklet of signals should include one which imparted the information that I had been steering boats for a few days and that my control, to say the least, was unpredictable. I was among the canoeists now and heading for the closest available section of the quay. The canoeists, whose ability at manoeuvring was considerable, weaved away from our boat whenever there was any remote danger of collision, but at the same time still continued their game.

One of the reasons for wanting to stop the night at Bourg des Comptes was that it was one of the relatively few places where we could fill our tank with water. My self-imposed dash for the nearest available mooring space had not taken into account how far the water tap was from the boat. It looked just too far, but there was only one way to find out. I grabbed the water pipe and went to jump from boat to shore. My initial uncertainty when moving round the cruiser had long since disappeared, and I jumped onto the platform, which sectioned off one mooring space from another, with confidence. It was one of the type which was not deep-rooted to the bed of the canal. I bounced down and then up. My momentum carried one leg over the platform and into the water on the other side. My other leg clung bravely to the platform, so enabling me to pull myself back. One totally wet leg and one dry did not seem the best condition to continue seeking drinking water. So I hauled in the water pipe, which was floating precariously near the canoeists, and returned to the cabin, defeated. It was the first time I was pleased that the canoeists were so involved in their game that they took no notice of what was happening around them.

After I had changed, I tackled the same task a little more carefully, only to find that the pipe was a few metres too short. We decided to go for a walk and, when the 'canoe-polo' was over, move the cruiser to a closer position. When we returned, we found that the canoeists had gone, but that other boats had taken all available spots close to the tap. Filling the tank simply had to wait. Just one of those days? Indeed it was. It was also to be one of those nights.

At about two o'clock in the morning I was awoken by a slow but steady drip somewhere in or near our bedroom. Thoughts of our recent adventure on the rocks sprang immediately to mind. I shot out of bed, unconcerned by my lack of attire, and checked the taps. They were not the cause. Eventually I found the source of the drip, under the floor of our bedroom. A board was lifted. Underneath were a series of pipes. Much feeling around led me to find the culprit pipe, under which I placed a plastic bowl.

Polly's most vivid recall of the event was the vision of my bare bottom sticking up in the air with much of the rest of my body under the floor. When I emerged there were many parts of me covered in oil or grease, though my arms and face were the most affected. Polly found the event extremely amusing; in fact she had difficulty in keeping her laughter below hysterical proportions. When she reached for the camera and started fixing the flash, it was time to do something I had never done before. I showered at half past three in the morning.

The next day further inspection revealed that the drip appeared not to be serious. However, we decided to use the emergency service available and so phoned for an engineer. The same engineer who had taken us through our first lock, arrived a few hours after phoning. He looked sceptically at us, when he saw who it was, and then apologized for being so long, as he had just finished dealing with a boat that had sunk. He added that this sinking was the first they had had since the company had opened. I declined to mention that it was nearly the second in three days. He then tightened a nut and reassured us we were in no danger.

While having a drink before departing, he told us in French of the intensive English course he had followed, when training for his present job. He had learnt how to explain in English the workings of the various boats used by his company, but had no idea how to carry out a basic conversation in English. He was competent in using this specialized language, a fact which could flummox those who believe that language should be learnt from a solid foundation.

We decided to eat before filling our tank and moving on. This delay proved a mistake, because as soon as the official French lunch hour had finished a wedding party came down to the river. They were intent on watching the boats. I was intent on not looking foolish. Therefore the difficult manoeuvring, required to put our boat in a good position to fill the tank, had to wait.

During this time we were disturbed by a drunken teenager who, having spied a bowl of apples through our cabin window, decided he wanted one. He tried to use charm at first, but I was unimpressed. Then he made a mock attempt to steal one through the open window. Further loud and unsubtle requests followed, until I succumbed and tossed an apple to his laughing girlfriend. 'Battening down the hatches' was the order of the day.

We were saved from total misery by a change in the weather. For the first time during our week grey clouds covered the sun. The drunk and his girlfriend disappeared, as did the wedding party.

Now was the time to fill the tank. My turning of the boat and guiding it into a very tight spot was achieved with near professional perfection. If only there had been a crowd to see it! Having already jealously watched others fill up with water, I knew that the pipe had to be hand-held to get any water down it. I also knew it would be a long job, for most of the water failed to enter the pipe. Undeterred, I put one end in the water tank and prepared to hold the other under the tap. It was then that it started to rain. It was gentle at first so I stuck to my station. Then a genuine cloudburst hit the village. Should I get my waterproofs on? Should I shelter in the cabin until it was over? We had waited so long for this precious fresh water that I decided to play the stoic. For a quarter of an hour I crouched by the tap, getting soaked. I had never felt so sorry for King Lear as I did then. The task completed, I squelched my way back to the cruiser. I entered the cabin well-doused and ready for my second, unscheduled shower in twelve hours.

Many of the unfortunate events that had occurred during our stay at Bourg des Comptes had stemmed from my efforts to conceal my own inadequacies. To attempt to hide failings is a definite form of dishonesty. However, in our society we are used to cynically criticizing failure, leading to such concealment being far more prevalent. Open self-criticism and total frankness are rare traits.

I did manage to display these qualities (along with one or two character defects), when returning to the company's base at Messac. During the week I felt I had mastered the art of going forwards. But command of the boat in reverse was, to say the least, inconsistent. Therefore I confidently steered the cruiser faultlessly forwards into a mooring space. Our now bosom friend, the engineer, walked down the jetty to meet us. He asked me to reverse the boat into a space. The one directly behind us was vacant. It seemed a simple matter. Unfortunately the boat veered away from the space. Forwards we went, to prepare for another attempt. Again failure! Four times I tried in vain, each time becoming more aggressive with my use of the gear lever.

My angry revving of the engine had brought out half a dozen interested members of the boating fraternity. It was too late to hide my incompetence, so for a change the presence of an audience became immaterial. I shot off to another place to park the cruiser. (I purposely use the word 'park' because a non-nautical term is more apt to describe my efforts.) As before, I was unsuccessful. The engineer now decided to give me verbal assistance.

'Right hand down. Left, no left.'

I was uncertain whether he wanted me to steer the boat to the left or move the wheel to the left. We proved not to be a natural team. His voice became more intense and I became more bad-tempered and unpredictable. The situation was soon rectified by the engineer jumping aboard and gently reversing the cruiser into its berth. At the same time I was relieved. It was not until later that I felt disappointed at my inadequacies.

Nevertheless the week was immensely rewarding. To be able to observe the hidden rusticity of rural France in slow-moving tranquillity was not to be missed. Highly recommended!

12

PEAKS OR TROUGHS

'Kate, you will have nearly learnt French by the time we leave here.'

'Nearly?'

Was Kate's reply said with serious indignation or sarcasm? I decided it was both. She realized that the range of her vocabulary was not great. But she also knew that using her limited stock of words, she could be mistaken for a French child. By Easter her keen ear had picked up all the local colloquialisms and her accent was impeccable. She was also able to reproduce the high-pitched tone that is a trait of French children.

Although Luke did not have Kate's determination to conquer the language, he too had made massive strides and was speaking fluently with his restricted vocabulary. He was able to cope single-handed with the work expected of him. Manuella's helpful prodding was no longer essential. He was even beginning to play the system. Monsieur Girardot was accustomed to setting homework in the afternoon and then going over the work done the following day. Luke was with a younger class in the mornings, to gain assistance with reading French, so he reasoned the homework need not be done. We did not argue and neither did his teacher. This honeymoon with homework did not last long, for his visits to the different morning groups were felt to be no longer necessary.

By Easter homework in general required much less assistance from Polly. The children were much more able to work things out for themselves. It was interesting to note, though, that the degree of difficulty in Kate's homework was far greater than Luke's. It must have been decreed that an academic approach to work begins at the age of nine in French schools.

Some of the concepts these nine-year-olds were asked to cope with were extremely complex. Kate was asked to create a framework for a technical project. Some of the sub-titles for this preparation were: project technique, determination of the need, creation of prototypes and analysis of constraints. Kate could not understand their meaning in English, let alone French. In France the National Curriculum asks children to deal with some extremely difficult ideas at an early age. They will then be required to practise these same concepts at regular intervals throughout their school career. Presumably it is the belief that at some stage understanding will eventually occur.

The National Curriculum also insists that there should be centralized testing. Kate was regularly asked to take a *bilan*. Much importance was given to the marks gained from these tests. Mademoiselle Gerard would read out the marks to the whole class in ascending order. This often meant that Christine's name would be read out first with an abysmally low mark. Christine was twelve and had been prevented from going to secondary school because of her poor attainment. Her duplicated year in primary education seemed to have done little to improve her ability. I cannot help thinking how demoralizing it must be for her to be constantly shown up in front of the rest of the class as having the lowest mark. It must have been just as soul-destroying that a nine-year-old English girl, who could hardly speak the language, was doing better than her in some areas.

The power of the National Curriculum seemed to have impressed itself upon parents and teachers alike. The test was of overriding importance. When discussing Kate and Luke's end of term reports with their teachers, all their comments were centred around the children's test marks. The way they were progressing and their attitudes while at school were of only subsidiary significance. The parents we spoke to on these occasions were also talking of marks as an indication of ability and enthusiasm.

It seems to me that this is a false premise. It is impossible to assess a child's progress by means of marks unless you have intimate knowledge of the marker's performances. One marker will sometimes unknowingly give more credit for presentation, the next accuracy, another might acknowledge content. The harsh assessor might give thirteen out of twenty for an assignment, whereas the lenient marker, perhaps seeking to reward effort rather than innate ability, might give sixteen for the same piece of work.

When we went to Kate and Luke's open day we were met at the school door by Christine. She had been working with Kate on some display material and was eager to show us the end product. With social grace she showed us around the classroom. She pointed out all the work they had done, stressing Kate's efforts.

I asked 'What have you done?'

She blushed shamefully. She pointed half-heartedly at a picture, then directed us to another area of the room.

'It's nice!' I said enthusiastically.

She turned to look at me with half a sparkle in her eye, almost seeming to scrutinize my honesty. She gave an unconvincing half-smile. She had been told how bad she was many times. My compliment was not going to change the conditioned opinion she had of her own ability.

'When are your parents coming?'

'They're not.'

We had become her surrogate parents for the day.

Christine's friendly attitude was simply one example of all the French children's approach to us. Their initial interest in Kate and Luke was not as if they were new toys, to be discarded as soon as the novelty had disappeared.

Luke had maintained his friendship with Manuella. To watch her walking down the corridor with an arm around his shoulder is something that would never be seen in a British school. The jibes would be too fierce to allow it. There was no amorous intent; she was merely being his guiding light. At the end of the school day Luke would often crane his neck upwards to give Manuella an affectionate goodbye kiss. He had not mastered the art, French-style, as she would invariably crinkle up her face and wipe the wetness from her cheek. Even so he was no longer horrified at the thought of touching or kissing other people. Indeed he was positively enjoying it.

Kate had established many friendships, yet she was bemoaning the fact that she rarely saw them out of school. Going round to a friend's house simply was not a regular part of a French child's way of life. The family unit catered for entertainment, therefore 'play' was likely to be with brothers, sisters or cousins. There was no chance of meeting at a public play area in Moncontour either, for there was none. The only play area was a private one attached to the camping site. Even the chance to get together for a birthday party never occurred. French children don't have them, well not in the expensive, all-embracing way they do in middle-class Britain. The family will honour the event, but without fuss and certainly without a special birthday cake.

To be invited to a relative stranger's house was unusual. So when we asked Manuella and her elder sister, Sabrina, to our house, we were astonished to find the two girls carrying a pile of gifts. There was a bunch of primroses for Polly (there is no law in France against picking wild flowers) and toys, books and sweets for Kate and Luke. If such generosity were to occur every time our children visited friends in England, our bank balance would be severely affected.

Kate and Luke were happily involved with school life now. One day Kate even insisted on going to school, despite having a chronic stomach-ache, something she would never have done in her first term.

On returning to France after the Easter break, Polly daringly said to the children, 'Let's turn round and go home. We'll make a start looking for a school, a house, jobs.'

'But we'll miss the Classe Verte.'

'I won't see my friends again.'

'I won't go back.'

Kate's face was a picture of stubborn resolution.

'I was only joking!'

They were not amused. Polly's assessment of the situation had been correct. There would be no heartache during their last term.

In the summer there were further signs that progress was being made. Kate intimated that in the bath she would often think in French when she pondered the day's activities. I asked whether she dreamed in French (I had been told once that to dream in a foreign language was a sign of being bilingual.) She couldn't remember whether she dreamed in English, let alone French. The evidence was inconclusive.

Before we came to Brittany, Polly had bought a couple of French for Beginners tapes to give the children a chance to grow more accustomed to the language. They never enjoyed playing them, and within a month of our arrival had totally rejected them. In the summer Luke played one of these tapes and listened to it the whole way through. Previously he had lost concentration after about twenty seconds, but now he knew virtually all the words and to listen to it was undemanding. His interest in it suggested he was monitoring his own progress. Kate dropped what she was doing to listen for a while as well.

It was not for long, though, for as soon as the Englishman who was introducing each section mentioned '*Être*' she gave a dismissive snort and walked away, saying in a mock English accent '*Et . . . re*'.

She had been scornfully discerning of English people's attempts to speak with a French accent for quite some time. When out of hearing distance she would often mimic British tourists' strained utterances. I only hope that when back in England her first French teacher is not one who had been cajoled into teaching languages because of the lack of specialists. A teacher with a wooden, anglicized accent would certainly test her patience.

Both Kate and Luke were now accidentally using French words and phrases when speaking in English. They felt embarrassed when they did it, despite our telling them that it was a sign of them being natural French speakers. Some words they had obviously used more frequently in French than English. Luke one day explained that he was going to have to recite a poem in class. Instead of the English pronunciation of 'recite' he said 'receipt' as the French would.

On being pointed out his mistake, he was openly shocked for he had thought he was using the English pronunciation. Kate used *cartable* instead of school bag. She realized her mistake and quickly tried to correct herself.

Despite this she faltered again, for all she could come up with was school sack. (Or was it *sac*?)

* * *

My own attempts to improve my French appeared to have a peculiar dependence on the seasons. After Christmas my language development, like the dormant fields around us, seemed in a state of abeyance. I was speaking less French than in the previous few months. The people of Moncontour were ensconced in the warmth of 'the family'. I felt I had reached a plateau, above which I would never rise.

Springtime brought a change. The serious, unapproachable faces of January and February had gone. People seemed rejuvenated. Conversations at the school gate became more animated, neighbours would stop and discuss; I was practising my language skills once more.

In spite of this, perfection was but a distant dream. Unpardonable mistakes were still being made. One of the most expensive was the time when I had made a last minute arrangement to play squash with Bruno. Because of the late decision we had decided not to bother booking.

When Bruno arrived one of my first comments was, '*C'est gratuit*,' hoping to mean, 'There is no problem, the court is available.'

His response was a most thankful, '*Merci!*'

I was a little puzzled at this, until I came to pay for my share of the court. I found Bruno had not gone halves as usual but had driven off without paying anything. When I mentioned the episode to Polly, she pointed out that I had suggested that it would cost Bruno nothing to play. I summarily cursed the English language for having two meanings of the word free. But despite my disgruntled nature, I refrained from phoning Bruno to ask him for the unpaid court fee. After all, how could I admit to such a faux-pas?

Another misuse of language occurred when two women knocked on the door early one Sunday morning. Even though I did not know them, I enthusiastically invited them in, trying to exhibit true, French-style hospitality. I was soon to discover that they were Jehovah's Witnesses. Whatever the benefits to my French a two hour conversation on ecclesiastical doctrine might have been, I was really not interested. Jehovah's Witnesses are renowned for their ability to maintain a conversation, however strong a rejection they might receive. How was I to persuade them to leave with limited knowledge of the language?'

'*Je ne suis pas intéressant*,' I said, in as politely forceful a voice as I could muster.

I was amazed. After looking meaningfully at one another, they left. I was impressed by my own powers of communication. That is until I heard Polly's laughter from the kitchen.

'You said you were not interesting.'

Polly paused to laugh again.

'They left, because you told them how boring you were. Could this be a role reversal?'

My self-congratulatory impulses instantly disappeared. To convert me to the cause was going to be such hard work that even the fanatical rejected the challenge.

Eating with a French family was a highly recommended way of practising the language. Unfortunately the linguistic proficiency was often dependent on the alcohol level in the blood stream.

I recall one such occasion:

First very large Pernod – careful and succinct;

Second very large Pernod – very talkative;

First bottle of wine with meal – uninhibited with creative sentence structure;

Second bottle of wine – quiet and monosyllabic (hosts are speaking faster);

Third bottle of wine – resorting to non-verbal communication (listening to serious discussion is such hard work);

Glass of Calvados – nectar-induced permanent smile. (Who's interested in the food surpluses in the EEC anyway?)

My failure to contribute towards the end of the meal had made me a little depressed. It was at such times that belief in my ability was low. I began to regret that I had not tried harder to become involved in some form of voluntary work. My children, when at school, had seven and a half hours a day of direct contact with French. I sometimes had less than half an hour.

I decided to do a language course. I chose a course in Brest, which was to last two weeks. So that I could be placed in the most suitable group, I had to complete a test unaided. I duly did this, and passed the end product for Polly to peruse. Her response was non-committal, a sure sign that there was no danger that I would be placed in the advanced group. She did mention, though, (after I had posted the test) that I had translated one phrase as 'I was awoken from my dreams' instead of 'I was awoken by my alarm clock'. Could thoughts of being part of the intermediary group be too optimistic?

Feelings of dejection were usually momentary, for I could see that progress was being made. I was no longer using a couple of words to try and suggest my thoughts. For the most part I was using sentences. I started to follow the instructions at my gymnastics evening class, rather than copy the person in front. I could understand the plot of my 'soap' without having to refer to the synopsis in the television magazine.

When we first moved to France, '*Oui*' or 'OK' was my nervous response to virtually anything. This habit started to diminish, but then I found I was using the words '*Bien*' and '*D'accord*' too much.

By the spring I had rejected these too, replacing them with a look suitable to the situation. This non-verbal communication, together with the occasional, undecipherable murmur or grunt, seemed to be an essential ingredient of French conversation. I was starting to adjust to this. The signs were good. Being in Brittany was gradually having the required effect.

13

REBIRTH OF A STUDENT

After the comparative security of living with my own family in France, the thought of going on an intensive course at a language centre in Brest gave me a certain amount of trepidation. No longer would there be the comforting knowledge that there was an able-tongued speaker of French ready to pick me up when I faltered.

The course required me to live with a French family during my stay. My family was particularly supportive. Their appreciation of the level at which I spoke their language was most reassuring. Rather than speaking to me at their normal, sometimes incomprehensible rate, they adjusted their speed of talking, so that I had every opportunity to understand. It must have been quite tedious for them, but it gave me a great deal of confidence and rarely was a word of English heard.

They also displayed the type of hospitality for which the French are renowned. They lent me a bicycle to get to college, would transport me to the centre of Brest when I wanted and indeed took me to Roscoff in time to catch the ferry at the end of the fortnight.

The meals lived up to all expectations. Breakfast was simple. Fresh French bread was the staple diet. This was particularly pleasant on the two occasions that it was still warm from the baker's oven. There was no sign of croissants or pains au chocolat. Perhaps they are not so widely eaten as the British believe. Could they be the equivalent of our 'full English breakfast'? The highlight of the meal was the large, Breton bowl full of coffee. I have always been a tea drinker first thing in the morning, yet to clutch a bowl of coffee in both hands, allowing the smell and warmth to permeate through me, was a really satisfying and relaxing feeling.

The college did not expect families to supply lunch from Monday to Friday, so my family adjusted their eating habits and, apart from weekends, had their main meal in the evening. Each meal would have at least five courses and was beautifully presented and cooked.

Sunday lunch was particularly memorable. An apéritif started the proceedings. Then, instead of the usual home-made soup, we had oysters. I thought this might be because they had a guest, but in fact they ate oysters every Sunday. Oysters are not my favourite seafood, so I have seldom eaten them. This soon became plaintively obvious, as I first struggled to open the shell and then began chasing the jelly-like meat around it in an unconvincing manner. My inadequacies produced some inoffensive laughter and genuine assistance to improve my technique. While we ate I noticed Michel pick up a shell and, like a sword swallower, pour the oyster into his mouth. This provoked a stare from Monique. The correct way to eat oysters was expected of him. When we all had had our fill, I was asked if I wanted to drink the water in which the oysters were prepared. I was assured it was good for the complexion. It was salty and unappetizing. My nondescript comment, that it was OK, was rightly considered as meaning that it tasted awful. So the water was shared amongst the family.

Next came some beautifully fresh salmon, followed by a salad and then chicken tenderly cooked with a rich sauce. After the main course came a full range of French cheeses, from the mild Brie to the powerful Pont Evêque. Pont Evêque is a cheese that can not only eradicate your taste buds, it can also maintain its presence in the kitchen, days after it has been consumed (or thrown away).

Wine naturally accompanied the meal. A disaster nearly occurred when the bottle of white had been finished, for Sophie had been poured the dregs of the bottle. There is a Breton superstition that if the youngest daughter drinks the last drop of wine from a bottle, she will be married before the end of the year. Sophie was horrified. Monique rescued her by finding two more drops in the bottle, which she duly poured into her own glass.

I tended to drink my wine more quickly than the others round the table and purposely held back, so as not to appear too greedy. I had a distinct feeling that wine would rarely have been drunk with meals, had I not been there. It is possible that the British have come to love wine partly because it is so expensive. Could it indeed be a status symbol of affluence? Could the French, on the other hand, because wine is relatively cheap, have rejected it as something to be savoured? The stronger apéritif seems to be more fully appreciated.

Fruit was the last course of the meal. Everyone had strawberries, dipping them in a central bowl of sugar, before holding the strawberry in the mouth and then ripping the stalk from the fruit. Coffee, untainted by milk, rounded off a delicious meal.

It is strange that such exquisite meals can often be shrouded by a cloud of smoke. Michel smoked during meals, as do many French people at home and in restaurants. It is a paradox, which surely will slowly start to disappear, as 'green' publicity begins to affect the less aware French public.

The eating of meals in France, whether in someone's house or a restaurant, has a unique atmosphere. Staying with a French family has a similar effect. For those who love the thought of being intimately involved in France, it is an essential ingredient for a true understanding of the people and their way of life.

* * *

The language course was to be orally based with some grammatical input. The course literature suggested that the speaking of a language other than French when in college would be a heinous crime. And indeed during the official contact hours this was so.

On the first day those new to the college were ushered into the library to be given information about the college's everyday routine and to be put into groups. (My test had put me in the intermediary group.) All instructions were given in French. I could understand some but not all that was said, as I am sure was the case for the vast majority who were there.

There was only one person, though, who was prepared to display her lack of understanding by unabashedly saying in English, 'I'm sorry I don't understand a word that you're saying.'

The promise to talk to her later was given, before the course organiser continued in French.

The voice that had echoed many people's thoughts was that of Lena, an English postgraduate. Her knowledge of French was minimal. She later stated that the reason for this was that she was a scientist. To mix science and languages in many British schools is extremely difficult. After two weeks Lena had probably made greater progress than anyone else on the course. Her determined, forthright, yet somewhat abrasive attitude in the beginner's group had reaped rewards. She had the right approach to make the most out of the course.

The lecturers admirably gave all instructions and explanations in French, only resorting to English if all else had failed. Like my family, they possessed the ability to adjust their rate of speaking to accommodate the standard of response. To have to do this for five or six hours a day must have left them in a zombified state, requiring some form of shock treatment to bring them back to the real world at the end of the day.

It was among the students that the English language came into its own. The Germans, Austrians, Swedish and Thais could all speak English and would regularly use it at break times if our French proved inadequate. It was not only the SOS language; it was also the communicatory bond between us. The only students who could not muster a second language were the Americans and British. To hear Matteus muttering a little Swedish to his left, a little German to his right, practising some French from time to time and then speaking immaculate English to the assembled group, clustered round their plastic cups of coffee, made me ashamed and extremely jealous. The other students' competence at English certainly emphasized the fact that it's the language of the world, making it very apparent why the British are so lackadaisical about learning foreign languages.

Being able to observe others on the course from a mature student's eye view was extremely interesting. I remembered quietly sneering at the lack of frivolity and dedication of mature students during my college days. I was now in a role reversal situation. In my group there were two Austrians and myself, who were obviously a breed apart. We were a picture of concentration, eager to envelop ourselves in the learning process. We exhibited bright-eyed delight when involved with some of the activities. When previously at school or college, talking was for giving instructions or passing on information, in order that we could write more convincingly. On our course conversation was the most important tool used for learning. To us it was an educational novelty to be enjoyed.

The rest of the group was under twenty-five. The vast majority of their lives had revolved around the education systems in their respective countries. This resulted in an outward show of apathy, similar to that which I wanted to show in my late teens but daren't. One German undergraduate, Skjell, excelled in this respect. His commitment to learning the language was at its most active in the bars and clubs of Brest. This resulted in eccentric attendance and a slouched attitude of hazy non-participation, whenever he was there. His thick glasses accentuated the effects of the previous night's activity. He would also take several seconds before answering a question. He would slowly pull himself into a position to respond and then drag himself back from his droopy-eyed dreams, before giving his softly spoken reply. I am sure his attitude had been honed at the back of a university lecture hall, for he became a lovable character to us all, seemingly defenceless to our regular abuse. He was our soft-hearted clown, unable to retaliate against the malicious tricks of his friends, and as a result he won over the affections of his audience.

Lise gained her credibility within the group because of her outward-going nature and her passion for organizing everybody's social calendar.

Everyone had her phone number and were given the same, 'If you want to go out tonight give me a call.'

She was American and described herself as a 'burnt-out yuppie', yet as our *après-college* organizer, she was far from burnt-out. She drew together all nationalities and types, giving every would-be isolate the chance to socialize.

Conversation was one of her great loves and this need affected her approach to language learning. In French she was unable to talk in depth and so she would often start a conversation in French and then revert to English to explain what she really meant. She would try every trick to get the tutor to respond in English, with limited success, so that the conversation would become more meaningful and exciting.

One big difficulty when learning a language is that, for the most part, you are only able to communicate in a mundane manner. For all but the last evening, I spoke to the two Austrians in French. This obviously assisted my attempts to improve my language skills, but it also made me feel that they were boring, shallow people. I am sure the feeling was reciprocated. It was not until the last night, when they succumbed to speaking English, that I really got to know and like them.

On most courses there is someone whose every comment jars. Karen, an English woman, aroused the metaphorical hairs on my back. She was usually first to answer a question, would think nothing of interrupting another's uncertain response and would openly show distain for a couple of members of the group, whom she obviously disliked. If she felt a session was going too slowly she would become temperamental, sometimes resorting to whistling to show her indignation. Due to the lottery of seating arrangements, I was often pitted with Karen when working in pairs. It was soon apparent that the subtleties of teamwork were alien to her. My thoughts were almost completely deemed inconsequential. Open argument seemed the only way to establish my point of view. I declined verbal combat, and as a result Karen concocted, edited and delivered our contribution.

I am sure that Karen's exaggerated assertiveness stemmed from a tenacious determination to gain as much from the course as possible. Indeed, like Lena, she succeeded, for of all the members of our group she made the most marked improvement during the fortnight. Her development was such that she was asked to join the advanced group for the final session of the last day. The progress she had made was a good example of how important it is to take every opportunity to speak in a foreign language. A shy, retiring linguist must be a rarity. To listen to the language passively will assist in the learning process, but active participation is the key to real success. Each time I was corrected when making an oral contribution during the fortnight, I remembered the proper version and could confidently use the expression again. I was less likely to retain other people's phrases.

If I had been asked to produce stereotyped cameos of the type of student I would imagine came from the nations represented in my group, the results would have been a long way from the reality. An American I might have expected to have been brash, insensitive and perpetually chewing gum. The gum was an ever-present feature, though Lise was perhaps the person most aware of other's needs. My English stereotype would have been sensitive and ponderous about total oral commitment. Perhaps I could have fitted in this category, but Karen definitely couldn't. The German would have been hardworking, intense and serious. The Germans in the group were some of the most laid-back people I have ever met on courses. My preconception of an Austrian as enthusiastic, yet relaxed, was quite close to the actuality. My expectations of a Thai would have been someone whose rigid, educational discipline would have left its mark. I would have imagined her to sit with a straight back, be quiet, indeed be the model of concentration and concise in her oral responses. Again my assessment was awry.

There were five Thai girls in the group, who were in the equivalent of the sixth form in a massive school of 19,000 pupils in Bangkok. (The numbers have obviously been limited as it is only open to Catholics.) For the most part they showed all the signs of being teenagers at the end of their educational tether. The lolled head, supported by hand and elbow, was commonplace and the use of folded arms as a pillow to catch up with lost sleep was not unknown. They were normally perky, relaxed individuals, yet during a session their eyes looked vacant and unresponsive. One attribute they did possess, though, which was far in advance of anyone else in the group, was an immaculate understanding of grammar. Orally they tended to be fairly reticent. Their educational upbringing had evidently stressed the grammatical aspect of the language.

The total destruction of any reliance I might have had in stereotyping occurred when I went with my family to a Thai evening, arranged by the dignitaries of Brest. It was to include dance displays, given by both Thai and French teenagers. The French children's dancing was modern and was treated in a fairly light-hearted manner. I expected the Thai children's dancing to have almost professional expertise. One or two of the traditional dances were exactly that, yet in others, the children made mistakes, smiled at friends and giggled behind hands. I was disappointed, for I had come to expect a more dramatic atmosphere to be created.

On thinking about it, I was pleased that my preconceptions

of Third World education had not been reinforced. Here were a group of human beings with faults and frailties, rather than robotic imitations of the same. Even my assumption that the dances would all be traditional was false, for the most effective presentation was a modern dance routine to pop music.

The final nail in the coffin of my Thai stereotype came when gifts were being given to the organizers of the Thai contingent. Ai, one of the students in my group, had been a representative for the pupils while in Brest and was to be officially given a hand-painted plate in recognition of the work she had done. Her name was called for her to collect her gift from none less than the *Conseiller Général* for Brest. There was no response.

'Ai,' repeated the exchange co-ordinator.

Many Thai heads turned in expectation. Two or three teachers moved quickly and anxiously to various groups of Thai children.

'Ai!' said the perplexed co-ordinator, this time more forcefully.

To stand on a platform and say 'Ai' every twenty seconds, trying a slightly different pronunciation each time can be a little deflating. The French 'organizer-in-chief' struggled to hide his discomfort. After the fifth or sixth 'Ai' there was a flurry of high-pitched conversation in the hall. The word 'Ai' like a bad dream, seemed to emanate from every corner. The French co-ordinator recovered his composure and took the plate from the unmoved *Conseiller Général* and placed it to one side.

In the morning I asked Ai what had happened. She blushed shamefully. She had not known that the gift was going to be presented. She had been less than inspired by the speeches that had preceded the gift-giving ceremony, so she had slipped out and was messing around with some friends outside.

I never became a regular member of the younger students' frenetic, evening social scene, though I was invited to join three of them on an afternoon trip to Quimper. Was this to be my chance to relive some of my more frivolous, student days? Lise, Matteus and I were to go in Lena's car. Lena owned a Skoda, which could be euphemistically thought of as full of character. When waiting for her to unlock the car, I stood next to one of the rear doors, giving the longer-legged Matteus the option of sitting in the front. Instead he insisted that I took the front seat.

Lise was also keen to sit in the back. I soon found out the reason was that they had driven with Lena before. Directions were needed to get out of Brest city centre, so I suggested that she turned left. The right winker went on and she stayed in the right-hand lane. (I later found that Lena had difficulties in distinguishing right from left.)

'Left!' I said, trying to sound dominant.

Her reflexes were in superb order, for she immediately accelerated in front of a van along side us. Then she veered into the left-hand lane, causing a car to skid to a halt behind.

'You've got to be positive in cities,' she dogmatically stated.

I considered asking her to elaborate on her definition of 'positive' but thought better of it.

Matteus, though, was keen to probe her philosophy of driving, producing such responses from her as, 'I always drive best when I'm on "pot",' 'I've had loads of bangs, but my car can take it,' and, 'I've thrown people out of my car before, if they've upset me.'

The last comment terminated this conversational theme, and all went well until we arrived in Quimper. Parking there proved difficult. Spaces were few and small. Our lack of success was noticeably getting to Lena. We eventually found a car park, with a space which was evidently free, because of an attractive tree at the far end. This meant that the car would have to stick out two or three metres. Lena drove forward into the space and, in order not to protrude too much, hit the tree. This was not though a mere timorous nudge, for the tree shook vigorously. The sound emanating from the collision was a deep, rich, metallic echo. Certainly this Skoda was made of quality material.

Rather than rushing out to look at any damage to her car (and the tree), Lena said, 'I meant to do that.'

'This woman will go far in the world,' I thought.

A pleasant afternoon was spent in Quimper before we set out on the return journey. Again I sat in the passenger seat. The conversation soon turned to the pros and cons of Skodas. Lena was very attached to her car and she made it apparent that our sarcastic comments were not appreciated. We were not in the mood for sympathy, though, and the remarks continued, upon which the Skoda's speed increased substantially. Now was the time to tone things down.

'No more tree jokes!' I said.

'Tree jokes?' responded Lise, not following my train of thought.

'A tree was the last thing she hit,' I replied, without thinking.

I tentatively glanced at Lena. Her eyes looked watery. Could this be it? Could my first attempt to relive my student days end with me having to hitch a lift on a French dual carriageway?

'There's a bottle of pills in my denim jacket. Can you give them to me?' blurted out a distressed Lena to the two in the back.

Tears were rolling down her cheeks now. Were these pills to give her a 'high', to counteract our insensitive remarks? Lise fumbled hurriedly through the pockets of Lena's jacket.

'I can't see a thing,' said Lena resolutely.

At about seventy-five mph that comment caused a certain consternation. Her pills were hurriedly passed to me.

'How many?'

'One! I still can't see.'

'Pull over on the right,' I suggested, handing her a tablet.

No sooner had I said it than I remembered the difficulties she had distinguishing right from left. I envisaged us parking in the fast lane. My arm shot out in front of her, in an attempt to hint at my meaning.

She rejected my suggestion and drove on. Her blurred vision could just make out the road but was not trusted to allow her to park on the hard shoulder. So we continued at diminished speed, straddling the two lanes. Her eyes were still streaming.

'I can't see a thing. Can you take the wheel?'

Her voice and manner were remarkably calm. I obeyed her wishes and steered one handed, while she manipulated the pedals. After a few minutes her tears receded and she was able to take the wheel again.

Lena's problem was not as I had first feared. It was simply a bad attack of hay fever. The attractive, yellow *genêts* on the side of the road had hidden, spiteful powers that had incapacitated her.

For the rest of the journey Lise, Matteus and myself were sympathetic and supportive. Four very meek people arrived back in Brest. The trip had been an experience. Rather than it being a means to recapture my youth, it became a lesson on the importance of sensitivity.

* * *

While on the course I kept asking myself, 'Have I improved?' Much of the time the answer was, 'No.'

One day in particular I was quite depressed. I had stumbled through the day's activities, sounding as though I should have been in the beginners' group. I was at my lowest at the end of the morning session, when the lecturer asked the group to create an extended sentence. The first person was to suggest a phrase; the next person was to repeat the phrase and add one of his or her own. I was to be one of the last contributors. The first few students coped easily, but the sentence was now becoming difficult to remember. The five Thais were next. Each one repeated and added to the elongated sentence with confidence and accuracy. I was amazed. My turn came. Not even the first phrase came to me. I passed.

I knew that people in full-time education would have sharper minds than mine, though I never expected the contrast to be so great. Was I suffering from a debilitating, premature senility? The fact that learning by rote was much practised by the Thais was of little consolation. I had had similar feelings many times in the previous few months and realized that it was a necessary part of the learning process. Deep down I knew that a morale boost would soon come, whether in the guise of a conversational gem or linguistic understanding beyond my ability.

That important ray of self-belief came when I returned to my family. When talking to Monique, I not only found that she was easy to understand, but that she seemed to be talking too slowly for me. I wanted her to speed up. (I did not tell her, though. I wasn't going to have my renewed self-confidence decimated.)

Other noticeable improvements were made during the fortnight. When I first arrived, listening to other students' less than perfect accents was laborious. I tended to switch off unless the lecturer was talking. Then after about a week, I started to tune into other people's conversations. Indeed I found that the French language was becoming much clearer. That fact that I had been listening to French all the time had enabled me to pick up the rhythm of the language, and in so doing the meaning became more apparent. It is like being at an Italian opera. When you are at one with the music, the emotional force of the performance will intimate what is happening. It matters not that your Italian is non-existent.

The most exciting development during my stay was that I started thinking in French. Unfortunately this was not a sudden transformation to fluency. Towards the end of the course there were a number of expressions that I would automatically use in French, without going through that painstaking process of translating from English. I had used them so often that they were coming naturally to me. Longer sentences and complex ideas still had to be worked out in English first. Even so it was a definite breakthrough, one I feel would have taken a long time without the intensive contact this course had provided. I was to stay two more months in France, to build on the foundation this course had provided.

14

SPACIOUS COUNTRY HOUSE – SLEEPS TWELVE

We had not gone to France to hide from our relatives and friends. Indeed one of our reasons for going was to be able to entice them over the Channel to spend a few wine-soaked days with us.

Before leaving for France, we had liberally scattered informal invitations to a mass of acquaintances. Among those were a few people who we were praying would not accept.

'Why did you invite them?'

'I'd run out of conversation. It just slipped out.'

'They'll come, you know.'

'No, they don't know us well enough.'

'You can entertain them if they do.'

An hour with such people was acceptable. A whole week would be a claustrophobic nightmare, prompting the desire for a nine to five job again. Luck was with us! We were genuinely pleased to see everyone who came.

There were no exaggerated apologies for putting upon us. There were no embarrassing silences when people were struggling to find another item of conversation. (One of the acid tests of a friendship must be feeling totally at ease in one another's company, even in moments of silence.) There was never that feeling that we were simply being used as a hotel. This may suggest that our friends' holidays with us were idyllic encounters, but this was not always so.

Ray and Julie's marriage thrived in England. They both had time-consuming jobs which minimized the contact time they had with each other. Being together twenty-four hours a day for a week proved a different proposition.

They arrived late evening, after a tedious day crossing and a tiring, fretful journey from Cherbourg. A glass of wine soon roused their spirits enough to recount the day's exploits. Everything was described to us in a frivolous, good-natured manner, until the time they took an uncharted diversion. Rather than simply explaining to us what had happened, they decided to rekindle the argument they had evidently had in the car. Ray had obviously lost originally and was eager to reinforce his previously limp responses.

If physical presence were decisive in determining the victors of such disagreements, Julie's comments would have been crushed into insignificance. Ray is a big man, and muscular, with a paunch of well-nourished proportions. He is fairly laid-back and normally quiet by nature. Julie is thin and angular, minute under the shadow of Ray's massive frame, yet she is a bundle of quick-thinking, sharp-talking, nervous energy. There was usually no contest.

On this occasion Ray felt that right was on his side; after all he had been driving while Julie was in charge of directions.

'Our map reader-in-chief managed to miss the Moncontour turning.'

Ray's sarcasm deserved a riposte. Julie immediately obliged.

'I told you where to turn. You were too dim-witted to react.'

'I'd have turned the car over, if I'd turned when you said.'

'You know what the French signs are like. You knew a turning was coming up. Whatever made you drive at that unearthly speed?'

Julie was right. You do tend to see some signs as you pass a turning, rather than before it.

'We'll go at twenty miles an hour in future, if it helps your map-reading.'

The remark was snubbed.

'Anyway whose bright idea was it to turn down a tiny track, that was sure to join up with the road we'd missed?'

'I was just trying to save time.'

Ray was on the defensive now.

'A pretty little farmyard we drove into wasn't it?'

The verbal combat continued for two or three minutes, until an empty glass enabled me to change the subject.

During their week with us I was invited to go on a sight-seeing tour in their car. It was an interesting excursion, as I was able to experience that peculiar feeling of not being sure where you are in a foreign country. Even though the map-reader (Ray on this occasion) could pinpoint our whereabouts, he was unable to eradicate that slight, indefinable feeling of insecurity aroused when venturing down rambling lanes, well away from the main roads. The quietness that comes with such uncertainty was destroyed when Julie took the wrong road.

'I said follow the road round.'

'This road has the same tarmac as the one we've just been on.'

'Don't be ridiculous!'

'The road you were suggesting was made of a totally different substance.'

A noisy, six-point turn was needed to investigate the scene of the crime. Julie's observations proved to be correct. So Julie won the argument, but Ray was in the right.

Ray's final comment on the map-reading sagas was to buy a car compass. He had a friend who had gone through London from west to east, using that as his only guide. This presumably was to give him and Julie the confidence to master the intricacies of the French road system.

Ray's most memorable achievement occurred when he and I had gone to the supermarket in Lamballe for a few items of food and some petrol. The first task was accomplished without difficulty. We then drove to the petrol section of the supermarket. Ray filled his near-empty tank up from the nearest pump and sat back in the driver's seat. He sat there for a number of seconds with a puzzled look on his face, before slamming the door.

He said, 'I think . . .' but failed to finish the sentence.

Then he drove to the cashier's hut, seeming oblivious of my presence. He paid and we started to make our way out of the supermarket. After about seventy-five metres the car started spluttering and jerking. It then stalled. Ray restarted it, and it kangarooed its way out of the car park and across the adjacent road, where it again came to a halt. It was then that he finished the sentence he had started near the petrol pumps.

'I've filled it with diesel.'

We walked back to check the pumps.

'Gazoil's not a brand of petrol is it?' he enquired, though he wasn't really looking for an answer.

The nearest garage was a quarter of an hour's walk away, so

I trudged off seeking assistance, leaving Ray to ruminate on his error. When I explained the problem to the mechanic, I expected a look of amazement, disbelief, something. Instead there was no change in his expression. The only inkling of a reaction came when I noticed an eyebrow being raised at one of his workmates. This I took to mean, 'English tourists again – easy money'. A different mechanic drove me in a breakdown truck to Ray's car (the cost of the error seemed to be mounting every minute). Before towing the car back to the garage, he stuffed a rag into the entrance to the tank and sniffed the dampened end knowledgeably.

'Diesel,' he confirmed.

I nodded.

'How much did you put in?'

'We filled the tank.'

This mechanic did not have the poker-faced attributes of his colleague, and a wide-eyed expression of incredulity enveloped his face. Ray seemed too dazed to feel upset by the finger of stupidity being pointed at him. He was probably more concerned about Julie regurgitating the tale at a future dinner party. We walked towards the pumps to fill the can with the correct petrol. The mechanic squirted fifty francs worth into the can. Ray and I searched our pockets for the money but we were a few francs short. Our patient mechanic reached into his own pocket for a fifty franc note, to save one of us paying by plastic.

At the garage a car they had been working on was immediately driven from a ramp to accommodate Ray's, the gazoil was removed and the fresh petrol poured in. Everything was completed quickly and competently. I had a horrible feeling that this preferential treatment might lead to an extortionate bill. My fears were unfounded, for the bill was a mere two hundred and ten francs (inclusive of fifty francs worth of petrol of course). I inwardly apologized for cynically misinterpreting the first mechanic's use of eyebrow.

Ray said little as he drove home. He looked crestfallen. He certainly did not appear to be in the sort of condition necessary to withstand the barrage of abuse we were expecting from Julie.

We related the story as soon as we got in. But instead of there being a verbal bombardment, Julie simply touched her arm with her hand and said nothing.

After bickering for much of the time they were with us, they spent the last two days of their stay with the same harmonious rapport as a honeymoon couple. Julie could certainly bark, but when given the chance to bite she declined an open invitation.

A week after Ray and Julie had left, I retold the story to Angela and Bryan over an evening meal. There was disbelief and much raucous laughter. I was as unsympathetic as the rest.

I remember saying, 'I think he deserved a real ear-wigging.'

The following day Laura and Charles, Angela's six and four-year-old children, were to be taken to Cobac Adventure Park. We had been there often and had a well-practised routine: a picnic in the grounds of the park, an hour or so's activity inside and lastly a drink in a bar overlooking the port at Dinan.

Everything went well to begin with. The picnic was delicious and the park invigorating (for some). As we were about to leave, I volunteered to go on ahead to sort out some drinks for the children, who were panting of thirst. When I was walking to the car, I felt in my pockets for the keys. There were none to be found. As I checked a second time, I noticed the keys lying brazenly on the picnic box in the back of our car. My habit of locking the rear door of the hatchback before I had slammed it shut (doing this saved me at least three seconds in time) had rebounded upon me. By this time everybody had returned to the cars.

'Have you your set of keys?'

'No I didn't bring them.'

'You're not going to believe this, but I've locked the keys in the car.'

'You . . . are . . . joking.'

It took ten minutes for the full ferocity of Polly's anger to be reached. During that time Bryan and I made some feeble attempts to prise our way into the car. Angela, seeing Polly's growing impatience, attempted to play the peacemaker. She had known many people who had done the same thing. The police were very good in these situations. Waiting didn't matter, the sun was still shining. As a mediator she had to be given maximum marks for effort, but as far as results were concerned . . .

'Has anybody got a coathanger?' I said without conviction.

'I've got half a dozen. Unfortunately I left them in our car.'

'Can you go and ask if anyone can help?'

'Me? You lost the keys! You ask!'

I felt Polly's superior French was essential in this situation, but my negligence had sapped what argumentative strength I might have had. I knew exactly how Ray had felt. I took back every scathing remark I had made the previous evening.

The nearest thing my bemused brain could get to challenge Polly's last edict was, 'What's the French for a coathanger?'

Polly remained grimly silent. So I disconsolately trudged back towards the park entrance.

As I was about to move out of sight Polly shouted back at me, '*Cintre*!'

I considered whether to ask if it were masculine or feminine but thought better of it.

I managed to communicate with the park attendants quite well and a maintenance man was sent for. I fear, though, that they were a little puzzled why I had this peculiar obsession with coathangers. A roll of wire was the maintenance man's coathanger substitute. Within a few minutes he had dexterously pulled up the button on the passenger door and so more costly solutions to the problem were avoided.

When on holiday it is essential to have something to do in case of unforeseen inactivity. Bryan's holiday hobby was learning French. He had bought some tapes, which he had played regularly in the car and was often found embedded in an armchair, practising various phrases. His headphones made him impervious to anything else that might be happening around him. At first his abrupt pronouncements were a little unsettling, but after a while we came to accept his laboured responses as if they were background music.

Kate took it upon herself to give Bryan private, individual tuition. They were regularly found huddled together somewhere, practising expressions. When speaking French, Bryan could never smile, his face was one big frown of concentration and his phrases were ground out, as if from a slow-moving concrete mixer. As a teacher, Kate was a perfectionist; the right pronunciation had to be attained before they could continue. She did not, though, have that precious teacher's gift of unassuming patience.

Her cries of 'No!' became more and more frenetic if Bryan failed to master a phrase.

Bryan remained tenaciously undeterred. He had only dabbled with French at school and had obviously fostered a deep-rooted urge to have a working knowledge of the language. I thought I was enthusiastic when I first arrived, but it was nothing compared to Bryan's vitality and resolution. He positively glowed after every success, however small. His first major purchase was his preferred brand of cigarette. The box was slammed down on the table, as proof of his achievement.

On another occasion he volunteered to shop for and cook an evening meal. His shopping expedition was an exciting adventure, particularly when buying the mussels. He had asked for five kilos and was a little non-plussed when the shop assistant kept shovelling the blue-black shells into bag after bag. Communication was needed to retrieve the situation. The non-verbal variety was dominant, and when this was starting to seem inadequate, he resorted to a more aggressive form of body language. He picked up one of the bags and poured the mussels back into the box from whence they had come. He then picked up another bag and with one arm clutched it to his chest.

'*Un*,' he said.

Understanding was immediate. He soon proudly walked away with one bag of mussels. The quantity was more in accord with our meagre appetites.

Another of Bryan's acquisitions did not prove so successful. He had heard much of the apple-tasting smoothness of Calvados, so he bought half a bottle. After dinner one evening, he sank into an armchair, warming his hands on a glass full of the whisky-based liquid.

His first sip produced the comment of 'Nice'. Subsequent reactions were 'Different!', 'It has a rough edge to it' and 'It's awful.'

Closer inspection showed that he had bought Calvados's equivalent of cooking sherry.

The language learning challenge was too stimulating for such setbacks to be a deterrent. He could well be taking the first steps towards becoming a Francophile.

Laura and Charles viewed France with a certain amount of mistrust, especially after I had dragged them along to pick up Kate and Luke from school only a few hours after they had arrived. Rather than meeting them at the gate, I decided to take them into school to show them what French classrooms were like. As we walked down the corridor, there was a babble of French conversation all around us. Laura and Charles's grip tightened on my hands. They saw Kate and Luke's classrooms but said not a word. They continued to cling to me.

When we got home, Laura intimated to Angela that she hated the school, and then after a pause for thought added, because they all spoke French. The comment aptly showed how insensitive an adult can be to a child's perception of things. I had not appreciated Laura and Charles's trepidation in treading in such unfamiliar territory. It certainly brought home to me how fearful and helpless our children must have felt during their early days in the school. Both Laura and Charles declined the offer of going to fetch Kate and Luke again.

Charles showed us how difficult it is for the very young to formulate the concept of a foreign language. Eight of us had squeezed round a table in a restaurant and were deciding what we wanted to eat. Charles chose sausage and chips, his favourite. Polly ordered for everyone. Charles had evidently been following her every word, ensuring that she ordered exactly what he wanted. As the waitress moved away from the table, his bottom lip jutted forward and he burst into tears.

'She didn't order my sausage and chips,' Charles blurted out, between bouts of sobbing.

We tried to explain that Polly had ordered in French, but he had not heard the magic words and he was inconsolable. Ray and Julie had previously shown considerable impatience when confronted with the French habit of taking their time over a meal. We started to feel the same way for Charles's tear-stained depression was total. A huge smile replaced his look of woe when his sausage and chips was placed before him. It was the biggest sausage he had ever seen.

The decisive factor as to whether we went into this restaurant was not the cost or type of meals available; it was the toilets. An advanced guard, Kate, was asked to go into the toilet and report her findings. Angela was insistent that if the toilet contained two footprints we were to leave smartly and find somewhere else. This type of toilet is much rarer in France than it used to be, but for Angela it brought back undignified memories.

The British seem to have an inbuilt fear of French toiletry habits.

An aged relative once told me she always kept toilet paper in her handbag whenever going to France. . . . 'You never can tell.'

The indiscriminate use of wall and hedge by the French male has long been a source of both ribaldry and horror in Britain. Norma and Keith and their three children, Matthew, Susan and Katy, encountered this habit when they stopped at some traffic lights, on their way to stay with us. The man in the car in front jumped out and proceeded to urinate into the undergrowth, unconcerned by the potential audience in the cars behind. Norma immediately attracted the children's attention by commenting on how unusual the markings on the brown and white cows were on the other side of the road. The children obediently looked with passive disinterest. Meanwhile the lights had turned green. The man was undeterred, intent on more important matters.

'What's the car in the front doing,' said Matthew, showing a true car driver's impatience from the back seat. The 'Oh' which followed his pointed question was said in an almost apologetic undertone.

Having completed his task, the driver unhurriedly returned to his vehicle. He did not even bother looking at the cars behind, let alone showing signs of humility or remorse. The spontaneous needs of a Frenchman must be answered whatever the disruption.

Norma and Keith were with us when a couscous evening had been arranged in aid of school funds. Eager to drink in all aspects of French culture, they were keen to join us.

I had already been to a meeting in which the breakdown of what should be eaten and its cost were discussed in never-ending detail. The most difficult consideration was what combination of ice cream, gâteau and cheese there should be. I have never known there to be such precision in determining the ingredients of a meal before. For instance twenty grams of onions were to be apportioned to each person. The estimated cost was four centimes. Looking at the final list of ingredients and their cost, I felt that twenty centimes per person for oil, salt, pepper and four spices was a little extortionate. I refrained from bringing up the matter, for fear of extending the meeting past the witching hour.

On arrival the first thing we discovered was that we had over-dressed. This was a truly informal get-together. The pattern for the early part of the evening had already been decided. The men stood drinking near the makeshift bar, while the women sat at the tables. Madeleine insisted that we joined them at their table, so after a couple of drinks we were ready for our buffet-style couscous. It was delicious. I could see now why the herbs had cost twenty centimes.

Conversation was difficult, as Norman and family knew a minimal amount of French. Carole had obviously been under orders to speak as much English as possible during the evening, particularly with Matthew who was of a similar age. She worked extremely hard, though she found that her English teacher had not prepared her for being able to understand strong Liverpool accents.

Half way through the evening I heard Madeleine ask Carole 'Has he spoken yet?'

She replied, 'Only with his mother.'

Madeleine's husband, Jean-Yves', first item of conversation was to admonish me for the order in which I had taken my drinks. I had started with a Ricard and then, feeling thirsty, had followed it with a beer. Jean-Yves insisted that they should be the other way round. The French will only mix their drinks in a specific order, one which the well-practised experts have deemed creates least havoc to head and stomach the following morning.

Soon after dinner, the band heralded the start of the dancing. Had we not been with the Hamelins, I am sure we would have happily watched from a distance. Madeleine and Carole's enthusiasm for it ensured otherwise, for each of us in turn was summarily whisked off his or her feet for active participation.

There was one dance in which everyone was involved. We moved round the floor doing something similar to the conga. In the middle was someone with a napkin, who enticed a member of the opposite sex to kneel on it, in order to be kissed four times on the cheek.

It was good, happy fun, that is until Madeleine was coerced into the middle. When it was her turn to grab someone, she chose Keith. Now Keith is a person who is not renowned for his outward-going flamboyancy. So to be on his knees in the middle of a dance floor, kissing a French woman, did not come easily. His face was visibly reddening by the second. Had he been watching what had been going on before? Around him were eighty or ninety French people who had practised this dance dozens of times. He decided that, if he were going to look foolish, he would not do it alone, so he chose Norma as his partner in the middle. Norma then chose me.

As I was making my way towards Norma, I could hear Polly's threatened comment of, 'Don't you dare choose me!'

While Norma and I were in the middle of our cheek-to-cheek embrace, Norma muttered through gritted teeth, 'For God's sake choose a French woman.'

I duly did her bidding and invited one of my gymnastics evening class to join me.

In the safety of our house everyone agreed that the napkin dance was the highlight of the evening. Norma felt that the evening was very similar to ones that often took place in Liverpool. It was lively, friendly and unpretentious.

Home-based entertainment was never a problem when Norma and Keith were with us. One evening it was decided to have a beer-tasting competition. There had been much discussion between Keith and Matthew as to which brew they should take back to England. They had been supping the four different brands we had in the house at the time (one was non-alcoholic), when I volunteered my services as organizer of the competition. Susan and Luke immediately became interested. So the four studiously sat round the table sipping the different beers, trying to put their individual tastes to memory. I rejected the idea of a spittoon, and Luke's impersonation of a drunk was not given its rightful acclaim, for this was serious business.

The test itself took a long time to complete. This was because Keith and Matthew had reputations at stake. Keith was a man of ale. He was knowledgeable, and critical of a bad pint. As a connoisseur, he was keen to see that standards were maintained and would therefore regularly visit pubs to ensure their beer was of consistent quality. Matthew had just turned eighteen and was a novice by comparison. Even so, in his few months of pub legality, he had worked hard to emulate the prowess of his father.

They sipped and pondered long. Keith's face was serious and unbending as the beer circled his taste buds. Matthew's, on the other hand, was a picture of concentrated determination. His forehead was deeply furrowed and his eyes rolled, as he strove to detect every taste sensation.

The results were difficult to read out without giving the glimmer of a sardonic smile: Keith one right, Luke one, Susan two and Matthew all four. Matthew contrived to hide his elation. Even so he positively glowed with self-satisfaction. Keith was quiet. He had even failed to identify the non-alcoholic beer. This was the time for polite sympathy. But we showed none. For the rest of the evening, both adult and child used him as the butt of our humour.

A glass of French beer nearly gave another of our drinking friends cause for concern. When in a pub Jon had found the feel of a pint glass (usually full of lager) as soothing as a child does a teddy. When Jon, Liz and Richard arrived from Roscoff, long drinks were needed to replenish tired bodies and frazzled nerve endings. As French beer came in bottles of a little less than half a pint, we were used to drinking from small glasses. When pouring the drinks, I found that we were one glass short, so one drink was poured into a pint glass. I decided this would be Jon's. As I stretched my arm out to pass him his refreshment, I was a little surprised at his reticence in taking it. He looked dejectedly at the beer and froth which failed to reach half way up the glass.

'Was this going to be my alcohol ration throughout the holiday? A third of a pint of beer every hour! Let's go, Liz!'

I too looked at his depleted glass and realized the problem. Back to the kitchen! Not only did I empty another bottle in his glass, I also poured my small glass of beer into a pint pot and topped that up with a second bottle. I wasn't going to appear a wimp.

Alcohol had what might be called a knock-on effect on Bob, when he and Jenny visited us in early June. After a lively evening of wine and banter, they prepared to go to bed in the dungeon. Bob, a tall man, had already ascertained how low he had to bend to negotiate entry through the low dungeon door. His confidence was such that he had discarded that awkward, crouched bend of a novice and replaced it with a fluent, unbroken movement. Unfortunately the combination of wine and darkness had tainted his judgement somewhat, and he head-butted the wooden cross-section of the frame. This was no gentle nudge. He attacked it as though he were a battering ram, causing the door frame to shake. With a little less poise, Bob entered the dungeon and after inspecting for scalp injuries, flopped into bed to enjoy an excellent night's sleep.

Jenny and Bob were probably the most professional travellers of all those who visited us in Brittany. Bob's work was drawing bits of aeroplanes. He was asked to do this in all parts of the world, so he and Jenny were used to dropping everything and moving to some foreign country for a few months. Despite this wealth of experience, Jenny made a cardinal error when coming to see us. She assumed that France in June would, if not sunny, certainly be warm. As a result she failed to pack any socks. Bob was an avid windsurfer and would seek out the windiest part of the coastline to visit. One day it was particularly cold, so Bob held out a pair of tartan socks for Jenny to wear. They were not colour co-ordinated, so Jenny instantly rejected them. Two hours later, having watched her boy friend sail above (and below) the waves, she surrendered to the nagging needs of her body. She put on Bob's socks, telling herself that if clashing colours were not fashionable at the moment, they certainly would be in a few months' time.

Towards the end of their stay, Bob offered to give me a windsurfing lesson. My interest in watersports is extremely small, but Bob's unabashed enthusiasm persuaded me to try it. First I had to overcome a mental blockage at the thought of donning a wetsuit. I had an aversion to the idea of it entrapping my skin. I also had a peculiar, hazy belief, that you needed to be over six foot and upright with muscular arms and a broad chest (Bob certainly came into this category – I hate him), in order to fit comfortably into one. When I tried it on I was pleasantly surprised. There was no discomfort, no sagging material due to lack of manly chest, and it was really warm. This was extremely important for Jenny was wearing Bob's tartan socks. As there was only one wetsuit, Bob nobly volunteered to enter the water in just Bermuda shorts, to give me instruction.

First Bob gave a demonstration of how it should be done. He mounted the board with ease, and, with a distinct lack of effort, slowly and gracefully raised the sail out of the water. Then with a brisk movement of his arm he was away. Simple! Only three skills to learn!

Needless to say I failed abysmally to master any of them. Each attempt resulted in me plunging into the water in many a varied fashion. Were I in a diving competition, I would have gained good marks for creative interpretation, though none for style. On occasion, despite tugging with all my strength, I even failed to shift the water logged sail. I was becoming hassled and depressed. Through all my tribulations, Bob was a calm, helpful, yet cold instructor. His Job-like enthusiasm remained unaffected until the water temperature defeated him.

'I've got to go in and get warm.'

At last the end of my ordeal.

'But don't worry! You carry on. Keep going for as long as you like.'

Then without waiting for a reply, he bounded off up the beach.

I had been making a small amount of progress before he departed. Now I was on my own, I reverted to my initial incompetence and, after five minutes, had pulled the board to the water's edge and strode dejectedly back to join the others.

As I walked in the wetsuit, I found I was able to reproduce that stiff, manly gait that other wearers possess. The reason for this was that I had a considerable amount of water inside the wetsuit and found it difficult to walk as normal. Although windsurfing did not appeal, I was becoming quite attached to Bob's wetsuit.

In truth I had found something quite compelling about my frenzied activities in the water, but the force of those feelings was not strong enough to want to windsurf again. I likened it to the time I had gone to fencing classes. I had been told to go away into a corner and twiddle the foil between thumb and forefinger. I had come to try and kill someone, so I never went again. My first windsurfing experience had not led to me being able to sail through the waves, so it was never to be an addition to my sporting bow.

Bob was soon preparing to go out on the waves again. He put plastic bags on his feet, which made me think that the cold sea had affected his brain. In fact they were there to assist him in slipping into his wetsuit, the interior of which had been inconsiderately soaked by the previous wearer.

Bob's love of windsurfing and his keenness that I should gain some competence in the sport led to another suggestion. He said it was difficult to do well in the sea the first time, because of the waves. He was all for finding a lake to continue the tuition on a smoother surface. My excuses came in a torrent. There were few lakes nearby. It would be difficult to find who owned any we might discover. I couldn't possibly allow him to become so cold again. My point was made and his optimism was crushed.

While watching Bob skilfully ride the waves, I asked Jenny if she noticed any flaws in my technique and what advice she could give me in the future.

'Give up!' she replied.

I did.

* * *

One of the things we didn't want to do when we came to France was to meet and get to know people from Britain. We avoided shops that publicised their English-speaking prowess and restaurants with *Angleterre* in the title. Of the British people we came across most appeared to have similar sentiments. They had a fairly laid-back attitude. They were obviously enjoying the more relaxed, slower pace of life, devoid of the sort of intensity that ulcers thrive on.

As in every generalization there is the exception. One day Polly was driving home after having dropped the children at school, when she noticed in her mirror a car that was following her around the twists and turns of the country lane leading to our house. Polly found this a little disturbing, particularly when the car followed her to our door. As she hurried for our inner sanctum, she was halted by someone calling to her in English.

'How long have you lived here?'

This question seemed to have skipped a few stages in normal, conversational etiquette.

Even so Polly replied, 'Since September.'

'I thought you'd been here a while the way you were driving around those lanes.'

Polly responded with a smile, hiding the fact that she had been driving fast in order to lose the car that was following her.

She dutifully invited the Englishman and his companion in for coffee.

Kevin and the girlfriend had been in France for eight months and were keen to 'dig out' any English-speaking people living in the area. He had spotted our car's British number plates and had ordered his French friend to make chase. He talked virtually non-stop for the next half hour. We heard of the various jobs he had had, how he loved France and the girlfriend's contraceptive problems. It was a potted life history. He spoke in a strange mixture of French and English. Easier words and phrases would be said in French. Then he would refer to English for more complex communication.

'We've been working avec battery *poules* since *deux heures, ce matin.* We're bushed! We were just going *dormir à ma maison.*'

Kevin's intermittent use of French was not an attempt to keep his work mate involved in the proceedings, for he directed all his conversation toward Polly and myself. If it had been, he would have failed, as from time to time his companion's head and eyelids started to droop, indicating that he would have preferred the afore-mentioned sleep, rather than the prolonged coffee-break. What Kevin was doing was to practise using French. It was the type of approach I would never have had the gall to use in company. This cheerful, outward-going attitude had obviously benefited him, for he had gained a good grasp of the language during his eight months in France.

This was particularly so as, to quote him, 'What I knew *en français* could be written on the back of a *timbre.*'

Having told us the intimate details of his past life, Kevin made as if to leave. He then suddenly remembered he had not got our telephone number. This suggested that we would soon receive an invitation to his house. We were wrong in our assumption, as he told us that he would phone sometime, to see when he could bring the girlfriend round one evening. This presumably was so that we were given the opportunity to practise French-style hospitality. As the two men left, I gave Polly that cross-eyed look of despair. We then proceeded to plan the inevitable social evening. Kevin had left the impression that he enjoyed his drink, so we decided to offer him and the girl friend at the most two glasses of wine. If we wanted more ourselves it would have to be drunk behind the closed door of the kitchen. This would surely persuade them not to make visiting us a regular part of their social calendar. For a while we expected every ring of the phone would herald Kevin's second coming. But the call never came.

We heard that he had failed to pay a bill for his car to be mended at the local garage. The garage owner was not unduly upset. He had mockingly dismissed both car and driver with a flick of his hand, saying that the car was a *poubelle* anyway. The next we heard was that Kevin and the girlfriend had unexpectedly left the district. Battery hens were an expanding business!

With the British and French authorities being so uncertain as to what our official classification was, perhaps we should have been considered as living in purgatory. I am sure that some people in France would class us as interminable tourists. Although possessing some touristic tendencies, I would have felt that in the latter half of our year the tourist tag would have been unjust. When we first arrived, we received that 'look' from the locals when we drove or walked past. Their heads would revolve ninety degrees to observe us on our travels. In the mirror I would regularly see clusters of people intently watching the car disappear into the distance. With the coming of spring their interest in us had all but vanished. There seemed to be an acceptance of our being genuine inhabitants.

As the summer arrived, I found myself reacting as the locals. I was no longer intrigued by the French, it was the tourists' antics that interested me. They wandered the streets with a hazy aimless air, eyes drifting in all directions. Their conversations, usually in English, was strange and somehow intrusive. Their clothing was generally garish and not always in accord with the weather. They had obviously brought their summer clothes and were determined to wear them, irrespective of the climate. T-shirt and shorts, in overcast skies with a biting wind, was one hardened holiday-maker's garb. Being windswept was evidently a sunburn substitute. But was this a mirror image of myself only a few months ago?

Probably!

15

BRITTANY – PAST AND PRESENT, WITHIN AND WITHOUT

Britanny's links with Great Britain should be strong. The Bretons had originally fled from Britain in the fifth and sixth centuries, rather than encounter the invading Angles, Saxons and Jutes. They named their new home *Petite Bretagne*. The Bretons soon excluded *Petite*, presumably for marketing reasons similar to the British people's decision to maintain the word Great.

In addition the Breton language has its Celtic roots in Welsh and Cornish. The names of towns, like Yffiniac and Carnac have obvious Gallic roots. Breton over the years has been successfully suppressed by the government. A few of the older generation can still remember a wooden *sabot* being worn round the neck at school as punishment for being heard speaking in Breton. It was only removed when the culprit denounced another pupil for committing the same crime.

Nowadays, there being more concern for traditional links with the past, *genocide culturelle* has been avoided. After much pressurizing of the government, *Écoles Diwan* were opened, in which about sixty per cent of the school day is spent speaking Breton. *Diwan* enthusiasts' statistics suggest that learning two languages at an early age assists in the understanding of all new concepts, especially studying a third language. Would bilingual primary schools be the answer to Britain's problem of apathy towards language learning?

In spite of undeniable ties, the modern Breton feels little filial closeness with his neighbours across the Channel. This is not surprising when looking at the callous way the British have dealt with the region over the years. Henry the Second was the monarch who showed the greatest disregard for Brittany. He, in an unquenchable passion, ravished Alix, a Breton woman. Had she been a mere peasant, it would have been of little consequence. She was in fact the daughter of Eudo and of noble lineage. Brittany was upset and took arms against Henry. The king proceeded to crush all resistance with unscrupulous severity.

The French capital has also not dealt kindly with Brittany. Even nowadays a Parisian will talk of a Breton in derogatory terms. Jokes are made about the stupidity of the Breton, in a similar way as the English will about the Irish. It is an interesting comparison. In both Ireland and Brittany much blood has been spilt, as a result of each trying to maintain its status. This often brutal persecution has been a major reason for both country's reliance on religion. Brittany still has the most strongly entrenched Catholicism in France. The strength of the family unit has helped ensure this religious commitment. (Religion is not part of the school curriculum in France.) It is interesting to note, though, that in Brittany relatively few people under forty attend mass.

The church is usually the centrepiece of the village or town. It will often have been built on high ground to stress its significance and to watch over its people. Evidence of how important religion has been to the Bretons can also be seen by a number of small chapels that nestle unobtrusively in the countryside. Many are still used today, but all can contribute an episode or two to the history of Brittany.

The Chapelle de St Malo was the nearest to our house. Its miniscule claim to fame was at the time of the French Revolution. A famous Royalist general, Boishardy, was raised in Bréhand. He had returned to the area to marry Grace de Kercadic at the chapel. A band of revolutionaries under the leadership of Audillas had heard of this and were lying in wait. He was shot three times, only a few hundred metres from the chapel. As Boishardy lay wounded, he uttered the word 'Grace'.

Audillas, showing true revolutionary commitment, duly gave him the *coup de grace* with his sword. Having triumphantly ridden into Moncontour, Audillas had a good idea. He ordered his men to return to the scene and cut off Boishardy's head. It was then implanted on a pike and paraded around Moncontour and Lamballe.

There is one traditional Breton, Catholic festival, the Pardons, which still takes place in many places throughout Brittany. The main aim is to seek forgiveness for all the sins committed in the last year. The occasion consists of a mass, followed by a hymn-singing procession around the town or village.

Each pardon is attributed to a saint, whose symbol is transported through the streets, as part of the procession. Moncontour's Pardon honours St Mathurin. The saint had been a great healer in his time, but it is doubtful whether he had ever been to the town. A small fragment of St Mathurin's frontal bone was brought to Moncontour, where it was embedded in the forehead of a silver bust of the saint. The piece of bone acquired a great reputation for healing.

At one time the Pardon at Moncontour was one of the biggest in Brittany, attracting as many as thirty thousand pilgrims, for it not only pardoned sins, but also ensured good health. All that was required was to pay a certain sum of money, touch the silver bust and then ring the bell in the steeple. People would even bring their cows to be blessed. A bell would be hung around their necks and would be rung, after the statutory payment of course. A mere two hundred attend the Pardon nowadays, suggesting that the effects of the blessing might not always have been successful.

Many who participate in the Pardons wear traditional Breton costume. This sadly was not the case in Moncontour. Even so the atmosphere created was memorable. Two services were held, one on Saturday evening and one on Sunday afternoon. The massive doors of the church were left open for all in the town square to hear the service. Even those who had stayed at home were given the chance of listening, as the service was transmitted through loudspeakers to every corner of the town. This was a new dimension to 'spreading the word'. Although the broadcast service would have invaded the privacy of a fanatical atheist, it was stirringly effective and dramatic. Both hymns and pronouncements seemed to boom from the heavens. The procession was sedate and in the evening, torch-lit. One of the directions it took was past the town car park which, this weekend, had fairground activity in progress. Some of the younger pilgrims, whose sins were obviously few, left the procession at this point.

Many of the 'Pardons' are used to attract tourists, and Moncontour's must come into this category. Alongside the fair two other activities were included during the weekend. One was a cycle race, full of sweat and fashion-conscious splendour. The other was the café waiters' race. Teams carrying drinks on a tray were to follow a course to all the bars and restaurants in the town, where they had to eat or drink something. Spaghetti was to be eaten without hands or utensils in one bar, its sauce, again using just the mouth, was to be drunk in the next and so on. All the participants were in fancy dress and few took it seriously. It was good street entertainment. The moment which will be the most remembered, though, was seeing someone relieving himself against a wall. I had become used to seeing men, legs firmly astride, studying the contours of the wall in front of them. On this occasion the man was in drag.

Along with the 'Pardons', the summer brought a large number of *fêtes*, from modest fairs to medieval extravaganzas. Brittany even catered for the more unusual event, such as a twenty-four-hour, fancy-dress tandem race.

Dinan's impressive, medieval weekend in October seemed to have the whole town dressed for the occasion. There were parades and street theatre, jousting and revelry. Stalls filled the cobbled lanes. It was a most spectacular, romantic glimpse into the past.

* * *

The French don't celebrate Christmas! This sort of statement can be heard in the splendid isolation of Britain, mainly I suspect because the French rarely send Christmas cards. What the French haven't done is become involved in the Christmas hype. In Britain the advertising machine suggests that Christmas begins in September. It begins in December in France.

In early December the shops in Moncontour naturally concentrated on Christmas, though in November there was not a sign of the coming festive season. Loud piped music set the atmosphere, though it was tediously unrelenting in its attempt to reach every alleyway. Every item bought, which was going to be a gift, was wrapped in Christmas paper for no extra charge. This was so, even in the large superstores, where two or three assistants' sole task was to wrap presents. The shops were delightfully attired, though the deer hanging outside the *boucherie* failed to impress Kate and Luke. When they noticed a straw hanging from the deer's mouth Kate, with a shudder, enquired whether it had been killed while it was still eating. Luke was particularly concerned in case it was a reindeer. Had it been Father Christmas's, this presumably would have meant less sleigh power.

Father Christmas's presence in Moncontour (he was there for a number of days) was a delight. He wandered the streets, talking with everyone and seeming to draw them together, almost as preparation for the coming festivities. Having introduced himself to every child, he would then dig into his deep, red pockets and produce a handful of sweets. From time to time he could be seen disappearing into someone's house. After about twenty minutes he would return to his duties, his red nose and cheeks rejuvenated. Indeed, by the end of the afternoon his whole face had a ruddy appearance. This seemed to enhance his generosity, for larger handfuls of sweets were produced from his pocket, one of which was frivolously thrown in the air for a group of children to fight over. He was certainly the spirit of Christmas. He was also eminently preferable to having to queue for an hour in order to enter some superstore grotto.

The mayor too showed his generosity at Christmas. He dug deep into the treasury's coffers, over and above the statutory street lights and town Christmas tree. At Moncontour School, ten Christmas trees were dropped off by a local authority lorry. Each classroom had a tree, as did most other rooms in the school. In Britain most schools will have the one Christmas tree paid for out of their own annual budget.

In addition the mayor hosted a 'let's meet Father Christmas' get-together for all the local primary school children at the town hall. The children were crammed into the room normally used for meetings and given juice, biscuits, fruit and sweets. The event was totally disorganized, yet remarkably there was not a semblance of chaos. Every child met Father Christmas and most would have shaken the mayor's hand. He was totally involved, talking to all who bumped into or pushed past him. In four months I had shaken the mayor's hand four times. In Britain I had never knowingly come within ten metres of a mayor, let alone spoken to one.

In order to show bonhomie to friends (sometimes enemies) and acquaintances, the British will have a party or drinks evening just before or after Christmas. Each house will have the festive feel to it, with a Christmas tree and eye-catching decorations. Occasionally lights will be hanging from the proudest tree in the garden, though it is rare for there to be an outward show of celebration.

In France the whole community seems to share in the joys of Christmas. Christmas trees are not simply for indoors. They adorn the streets, whether in pots or tied to drainpipes. They are like tinsel-fingered hands, open and welcoming.

Imagine most British families' reaction to the suggestion of placing a Christmas tree outside the front gate.

One of the most likely responses would be something like, 'You won't find it there in the morning!'

There are no such thoughts in France. Open house can be taken literally, throughout the festive season. The French do not welcome you by appointment. People can and do pop in at any time (except during the sacred lunch period) and receive the same hospitality as they would throughout the year. The only difference is that at Christmas they are likely to play host more often.

For those towns and villages who will organize one, the *crèche vivante* is another sign of the community pulling together at Christmas. It is a moving tapestry of the story of Jesus. We saw one in St Hillion, and it was tremendously effective, putting any nativity play I have seen to shame. The story was told over a microphone, alongside some sombre rather than joyous music. The actors (ranging from an eighty-six-year-old king to children below ten) mimed the event in majestic slow motion. The atmosphere was enhanced by a real donkey, cow and sheep. I, secretly and shamefully, wanted the lamb to leap from the little boy's arms or the donkey to dig his heels in and refuse to move, but the sense of the moment prevailed and there was no such discord. The only sign of the magnificent atmosphere being dented was the occasional sneeze and strangled cough of Mary. Her pale and holy face had not been created by astute make-up, but by the fact that she had flu. Despite my cynical asides, the event was totally compelling and gave a strong feeling of the true significance of Christmas. It was an immaculate conception.

The two important days at this time of year, Christmas and St Sylvestre or New Year's Eve are the exceptions to this 'open house' rule. The French are keen to point out the difference between the two: Christmas is for family, New Year's Eve and New Year's Day are for friends. At Christmas the extended family and an extended dinnertime are the reality. The abundance of good food and drink becomes even more important than conversation. New Year's Eve is party time, as in Britain, with the first day of the new year taken up with more formal celebrations.

The festive spirit infiltrates into January also. On the first Sunday after New Year's Day, to celebrate Epiphany, people will get together to share a *galette des rois*. This is a crusty pie with an almond paste filling. Hidden in the *galette* is a bean or china or plastic figure, in a similar way that a sixpence was a necessary ingredient to a Christmas pudding. The person who gets the object wears a golden, cardboard crown. The eating of these *galettes* can take place throughout the month. Luke had already won a crown and a miniature, plastic football during school dinners, when we bought a *galette des rois* for our own consumption. The package promised a bean. For three days we munched our way through the *galette*, but there was no bean. Thoughts of getting our money back subsided as the absence of the bean was a mite difficult to prove. The consumption of the *galette des rois* seems to be the only time the French come out of hibernation in January.

During our stay we took every opportunity to see as much of Brittany as possible. The medieval towns had tremendous appeal: Vannes with its canal and narrow, cobbled streets; ancient Quimper, a big tourist draw with its lanes and splendid cathedral; Morlaix with its audacious viaduct and steep inclines, and Pontivy with its river and impressive castle battlements. Dinan, though, was my personal favourite. The medieval centre of the town is exquisite. The many attractive shops, although catering for the tourist trade, have not succumbed to plastic mania. A part of Dinan that can easily be missed is the port. It crouches gently in the valley, guarded by a towering viaduct. It was our place to sit, drink and contemplate.

One of the most striking landmarks is Mont St Michel, situated in Normandy. It magnificently imposes itself on the contrastingly flat countryside nearby. We visited it with Allen and Denise on their way to catch a ferry in Caen. We entered the car park, costing ten francs per car, and stood together gazing at its sumptuous boldness.

'Right I've seen it! Let's go!'

'But you've just paid ten francs. Don't you want to go inside?'

'No, we've got a ferry to catch. It's very nice.'

They had plenty of time to catch their ferry, but Allen had that understandable fear of missing it. Being stranded in a foreign port is an uncomfortable thought and leads many people to arrive hours before they are due to depart.

So the four of us were left to climb the steep lane of Mont St Michel unaccompanied. Allen had made the right decision. The place was full of tacky gift and sticky food shops. It was a tourists' honeypot.

The children loved the coast. We usually chose to visit at midday. At that time the French were packing up in preparation for their main meal. The beaches virtually belonged to us. Our two favourite beaches on the Northern coast were at St Cast le Guildo and a little bay close to Cap Frehel, which had every adventure in its dunes, sand and rocks. Cap Frehel itself is the antithesis of its neighbouring, sandy bay. It is a steep headland with granite rocks beneath. On a clear day the Channel Islands can just be seen; in a fierce wind it is dramatically destructive, venomously breaking up the waves' incursions into the shore. Cormorants man the rocks, like satanic voyeurs, lustful for destruction, keen to watch the battle of the elements. The Quiberon peninsula on the west coast is just as wild, though it seems more stark and neglected.

The most austere place to be in Brittany must be among the menhirs of Carnac. Winter is the time to visit these massive stones. Even a handful of tourists can ruin the atmosphere.

Like Stonehenge there are many tales as to how and why the stones were placed there. A most popular myth was that they were sleeping giants who were aroused at certain times of the year to replenish their thirst. The story has never been substantiated, as anyone who sees them come to life is mercilessly killed. Most of the stones are upright, though some are placed at a slant. These were deemed to be phallic symbols and were thought to possess the power of fertility. Childless women would slide down or rub their naked bodies on the stones to become pregnant.

Many other menhirs are scattered throughout west Brittany. At La Guerche-de-Bretagne, where there are a series of huge stones, the first pre-marriage counselling service took place. Under a new moon, engaged couples would walk in opposite directions around the stones. Their task was to count them. If the lovers' tally was the same, they were assured a happy marriage. If there was a disparity of more than two, there would be marital disaster.

When in west Brittany we stayed at a hotel renowned for its special health section, in Carnac-plage. It gave advice and therapy and boasted a salt-water swimming pool. When we first swam in the pool, we were surprised to find that in France it was compulsory to wear bathing caps. The French nit must be more durable than in Britain.

The dining room was a little unusual as it was divided into three: for smokers, non-smokers and an area for the health section guests. I inquisitively looked into the health section's dining area and felt that nobody appeared to be enjoying their salad-based meals. It seemed hard for the red, meat-eating French to put aside habits of a lifetime.

Before coming to France we thought that French people's keenness for meat might be a problem, particularly for Luke. In England he had become a vegetarian (a difficult thing for him to do as he had enjoyed the taste of meat). On our first excursion to a hypermarket both Kate and Luke were horrified that horsemeat was on sale and that chickens and rabbits looked uncommonly like their former selves. I foresaw school dinners causing a certain amount of difficulty.

The school dinner ladies insisted that the children ate everything in front of them, so Luke, unable to argue, resigned himself to eating meat again. He enjoyed this renewed acquaintance. One day he asked one of the dinner ladies what a certain meat was.

She said, '*Mouton*,' and pointed at her tongue.

Sheep's tongue became his favourite delicacy in France. Whatever else the year abroad did for Luke, it definitely changed his eating habits.

Unlike Normandy, Brittany does not have a renowned reputation for its food. It is best known for its seafood,

Coquilles St Jacques being the most famous. There is another Breton seafood dish though, which is thought by many to come from the United States. *Lobster à l'américaine* is often seen on menus. It should read *lobster à l'armoricaine*. Armorique was the original name for Brittany. (*Armor* means sea in the Breton language.)

Crab was another seafood speciality we tried. There is something ostentatiously splendid about a meal that incorporates an animal that is virtually in its original state. Luke liked potted crab and had been longing for some time to enjoy the real thing. We surrendered to his nagging pressure and when on a trip to Finistère, we specifically went to a seafood restaurant, for the sole purpose of introducing him to crab. The choice of restaurant was difficult, as Kate did not want one where you choose your meal from a tank.

The idea of Luke saying, 'Look how quickly that one moves. Isn't its shell pretty! I'll eat that one!' was not going to help her appetite.

A suitable restaurant was found and Luke's crab was ordered. The delight on his face, as it was placed before him, was immense. Normally Luke is fairly slouched when he eats. On this occasion his back was straight with pride. Unfortunately the surgical instruments used to disenrobe the crab, for the most part, were too difficult for him to utilize. This was a disappointment, for Luke likes to eat quickly. Very little flesh seemed to come out of this big crab. This was a disappointment too for Luke enjoys large meals. In the end the thought was better than the actuality. He decided to stick to crab from tins in future.

The *crêpe* (made with white flour) and *galette* (made with black flour) are very popular in Brittany. The rolled *crêpe* can often be seen eaten as a snack, especially on market day.

A visitor should not miss the chance of eating in a *crêperie*. The biggest problem is that one *crêpe* is seldom enough. It seems to leave you hungrier than you were at the start of the meal. Experimentation over the wide variety of fillings (I particularly liked rhubarb and nut) becomes a must. The effects of a *bolée* or two of traditional cider (it can be as mellow and lethal as scrumpy) can lead to a procession of *crêpes* being devoured. The bill at the end of the meal can be as deadly as cider.

* * *

Paris was too far away for us to make visiting a habit, yet it would have been unpardonable to disregard it altogether. As a family we went there three times and were never disappointed. The journey by TGV took three hours, yet the family areas of the train were spacious, and we travelled in a comfortable, unhustled manner, with no more than the gentlest of sways to suggest we were moving at all.

The pace of Parisian life was hectic by comparison with the smooth train journey. Those who use Paris to work or live in step out purposefully. Theirs is often a dour expression, showing a total disregard of all that is happening around them. They appear to have obliterated the outside world from view, concentrating on getting to their destination as quickly and untroubled as possible.

It is probably this, more than any other aspect, that has helped to characterize the Parisian throughout the rest of France. He is thought of as cold, uncaring, superior and often rude. If I constantly had to endure the packed streets, métro and buses, I would react similarly. The rush hour traffic jams are just as frustrating, like those found on the *périphérique*, a more chaotic equivalent of the M25. The only way to remain sane, amid the noisy fracas of Paris, is to close your mind to its existence. I met a Parisian, now living in Brittany, who said that he loved Paris, as long as he did not have to live there. Many Parisians have similar sentiments. Having been lured away from the restrictions of family life to enjoy more varied work prospects, it was found that over half of these newcomers to Paris would now prefer to live elsewhere.

The people in the provinces are unaffected by such *cris du coeur*, and the Parisian is considered a different breed. I was once told that the Bretons liked best to sell their houses to the British, then the Germans and lastly the Parisians. Paris has been less than supportive of its provinces in the past and obviously traditional hatred still runs deep. It will take a long time for these attitudes to change.

Despite the rest of France's disenchantment, tourists are captivated by the ambiance of Paris. Psycho-therapists should set up in business in a Parisian bar. Treatment would simply consist of watching the world go by. The smart and the strange, the outrageous and the deprived will all parade for you. Taking in this show, together with an inimitable coffee or beer, must be one of the most satisfying, passive hobbies in the world.

Having 'done' Paris many times before, I found I had more time to consider the individuals who coloured the streets, five young people hurried from a nearby car. They carried cans of paint spray, which they smartly placed on the pavement near a shop's closed, metal shutter. Three of them started spraying the shutter, not haphazardly, but with preconceived certainty. The operation was being carried out with almost military precision. One took the role of look-out, while the other, notebook in hand, supervised proceedings.

There are many ugly slogans daubed on walls in Paris. This street art, though, is a more sophisticated graffiti. Rather than scrawled displays of hopelessness, the spray painters are making a positive reaction to the system.

They are saying, 'Look! We have talent! Give us a chance!'

The artists dotted along the banks and bridges of the Seine exude a different temperament. They are serene, almost docile, yet their minds are constantly active, as they study their composition. Then with a deft movement of the wrist, an image is uncannily recreated, by a mere flick of the brush or confident squiggle of the pencil. The hot chestnut seller also works with the minimum of fuss and movement. His concentration is in pushing and turning his chestnuts. The comments and sighs of the paying public have long since lost his interest and he barely acknowledges their presence.

The African sellers of belts, bags and trinkets seem to divide themselves into two types. There are the hugely patient, statuesque sellers, whose pride prevents them making an untoward suggestion. Then there are the aggressive salesmen who will endeavour to catch your eye. Having done so, they will quickly move towards you, head slightly bowed, and try and entice you to peruse their wares. I cannot remember seeing anyone busy from these stalls. Their profit margin must be very slender.

These are but a sprinkling of the wide variety of characters who abound in Paris and help to give the city its unique magnetism.

16

CLASSE VERTE

'Here's a roll of bin liners. You'll need them on the trip.'

I was puzzled into silence.

'You're travelling from Britanny to the Auverne by coach. They're essential.'

I was starting to follow Polly's thinking.

'We've got couchettes. They'll be sleeping most of the way. Anyway you hardly know you're moving on these modern coaches.'

'You'll regret it.'

'And there'll be a toilet.'

'Do you remember the time when. . . ?

Polly had greater experience on coach trips, and the thought of her being right, without any counter-measures available, was horrifying. So the bin liners were squeezed into my hold-all.

* * *

Every four years, a school has the opportunity to take children to another part of France on an activity week. There are a wide variety of courses, such as *classes de neige*, *classes de mer* and *classes vertes*. The latter was chosen by Moncontour School.

Kate and Luke were of the right age to go. Volunteer helpers were needed; so ever eager for contact with the language, I offered my services.

The luxury coach had been luxurious ten years previously, and therefore the smooth ride I was expecting was distinctly absent. I had been impressed by French roads until this trip. Every bump and camber transmitted themselves to me. The headrest pillow failed to give, and my head bounced gently throughout the normal hours of sleep.

These uncomfortable sleeping arrangements did not seem to upset the children. Three or four did have stomach ache as we encountered the winding roads near the Loire; but it was not until Luc-Thomas made a quick dash for the toilet that our real problems began. Luc-Thomas has an ability to over-emphasize. A comment of outrage would quieten a canteen, a sneeze would interrupt people's lines of thought. Similarly his dissatisfaction with the movement of the coach had a remarkable effect. In his hurry to reach the toilet, he had left the door open, allowing his lengthy criticism of the coach's girations to echo throughout. People's responses on this occasion were more dramatic than mere silence. A chain reaction worked its way fore and aft of the toilet. I unravelled bin liner after bin liner, passing them quickly to every stricken child. Few finished the journey unscathed.

Luc-Thomas soon became the butt of the adults' jokes at the activity centre. He had the ability to produce the totally irrelevant question.

Instructor: 'These are Aubrac cows.'

Luc-Thomas: 'Who lives in that house in the valley?'

His questions were frequent and spontaneously fired with an open-eyed eager naivety. They soon became wearing and were often rejected with sarcastic disregard.

He remained undeterred, though, and as soon as his imaginative brain had conjured another mystery, his '*Monsieur, monsieur, monsieur*' would interrupt any instruction or explanation.

Each mealtime Luc-Thomas would pop up from his seat two or three times to receive a reassuring answer to a burning question. He was impervious to comments about such things as there being more peas around his plate than on it, and the fact that he had used the letter he had written to his parents as a serviette to remove soup from his hands. His imitation of a technically correct, golfing stroke deposited eight marmalade dishes, that the kitchen assistant had carefully balanced in her hand, to all parts of the dining area. In adolescence he might well grow to use his natural innocence for more devious forms of attention-seeking, but for the moment his unco-ordinated play-acting was a light-hearted entertainment.

As the manager of the activity centre said, 'Every group has one.'

French children do not differ from their British counterparts. Blanket stereotyping cannot be used, for individual characters abound.

There was Jean-Pierre, with a short-term memory. Shoes, towel and money pouch were lost and found in unusual places. He left his kagoule behind three times, once at the top of a mountain. Unfortunately he did not realize until he had reached the bottom. This necessitated a disgruntled Monsieur Girardot trekking back to retrieve it.

There was Gurvan, a tiny, impish boy. He spent much of his time on his knees, scrummaging in the undergrowth for frogs and grasshoppers, spiders and most especially slugs. The slug population of the Auverne is obviously well-nourished and this fascinated him. He was often seen examining the size of his latest find. His fingers would measure the length and girth of each discovery. The only English word he wanted to learn during the week was 'slug'. I heard him practising it hours later, before he went to sleep. Even on the coach journey home he was lying on the floor, fingering dust as it floated through the sun's rays.

There was Patrick of the thousand scrunched faces. He sought rather than paid attention. He would enter a room with a straight-legged, stamping walk and an expression suitable for the occasion. He wore his kagoule backwards and his sun hat in all manner of ways. He would distract and subsequently attract the weary minded.

There was Anne-Sophie with no close friends. She was fat, slow-thinking and with a speech impediment, yet she had magnificently come to terms with her apparent lack of assets. She rolled her way through the week, scoffing her own limitations and becoming involved in everything. Her enjoyment was total. She probably got more out of the week than anyone else.

There was Dominique who, by contrast, was attractive and very capable. She continually forced a charismatic image on her would-be friends, but her displays of bravado were false and sometimes embarrassing. She continued to be rejected. The continuous rubbing of her left eye, making it very sore, brought teachers, instructors and helpers to her side, trying to comfort her and brighten her waning spirits. The following day there proved to be no infection in her eye, although it was still red. Was her problem tiredness or an inner cry for affection?

It is very difficult for teachers or instructors, even with a first aid certificate, to diagnose the difference between a mild and a serious, medical condition. With late nights and testing physical demands, came stomach complaints and lethargy. Julianne had stomach pains which developed into vomiting. Two or three inconclusive discussions took place, before it was decided to send for the doctor. The fact that Karine had badly grazed and bruised her back on a rock face and had difficulty in walking was one of the determining factors in the decision. Julianne was given an injection and spent a day in hospital with suspected appendicitis. Happily it was a false alarm.

Another group of teachers might not have called the doctor.

'What sort of personal insurance do the parents have? (Our trip was not specifically covered.) One of the staff will have to stay behind with her and the activities would not be properly supervised. Think of all that form-filling. It's probably just a tummy ache!'

Thoughts like these could easily have led to a 'wait and see' policy.

At first sight the cost of medical help looked extortionate, though personal insurance would have covered most eventualities. For the doctor to be called out Karine and Julianne's parents would have sought ninety francs from their respective insurance companies; Julianne's injection cost one hundred and nineteen francs, though additional charges would probably have been incurred for special medication etc. Monsieur Girardot's premature baby's twenty-three day stay in hospital cost twenty-three thousand francs. It is certainly worth putting your medical insurance on direct debit.

Despite there being a number of niggles through fatigue, there was a good collective spirit throughout the week. There were no disruptive cliques and, in spite of one or two children being fairly isolated, there was no vindictive spitefulness.

Even so some of the more emotional outbursts tested the teacher's ability to mete out justice with sensitivity. When Jacqueline and Caroline sat defiantly opposite one another, refusing to continue on the bike ride through the forest, skilful intervention was needed. Everyone had dismounted for a five minute rest, leaving the bikes clattered together on a nearby bank. As the cyclists prepared to delve further into the forest, the two girls were embroiled in a 'tug-of-bike' competition. Jacqueline won, so Caroline sat stubbornly on a rock, her face tear-flecked. She then started to give Jacqueline an uncontrolled, verbal pounding. I was the nearest adult.

'Come on! Let's go!'

My rather feeble suggestion stemmed neither Caroline's flow of conversation nor tears. I then decided on the subtle approach and started admiring the merits of the untouched bike. (Unfortunately it was exactly the same model as the one being contested.) Had it been a Hinault cast-off, my efforts would have been in vain. The bike itself was immaterial by now, it was merely a symbol of victory. Jacqueline was losing the emotional battle, so she too began to produce a mixture of tears, sobs and abuse.

The instructor swiftly came to my assistance. She started talking about everything other than bikes. At the same time she began readjusting their brakes, gears and saddles. Soon the girls stopped talking at one another and started talking with the instructor. Their faces still showed true martyrdom, but the storm had passed and Caroline mounted the unwanted bike albeit morosely.

Patrick also declined to continue, when on one of the hill climbs. He lay on the grass, complained of tiredness and resisted all reasonable methods of persuasion to get him on his feet. He had been dancing his way between the trees for most of the walk, showing no signs of fatigue. So his stubbornness had to be an act of rebellious showmanship. I am sure it was a result of our dining room conversations over the previous two days that prevented any of the staff from lifting him to his feet and forcibly marching him on up the hill.

In those two days all that anyone had seen Patrick eat were two chunks of bread. Soup, meat, vegetables, cheese, fruit had all been declined. There had been talk of malnutrition, phoning his parents, even threatening to send him home. All forms of cajoling had failed to get him to eat any of the healthy food provided.

Could Patrick's demise on the hillside be attributable to lack of nourishment? Was this the beginning of a serious health problem? I volunteered to stay with him while the others continued the climb. If he didn't want to catch up with the rest, I would walk with him back to the activity centre. Patrick's best friend's request to stay with us, because he had suddenly developed an ankle problem, was summarily rejected.

I decided to bore him into submission. I asked him what his parents did, about his brother and sisters, where he lived. Questions like these were interspersed with comments of how small the others looked in the distance and what a marvellous view they must have. Then I asked him what his favourite sport was, ready to follow it up with how important it was to develop stamina in whatever activity he suggested. I did not understand his reply, so I asked the question again. He must have realized that I had ulterior motives, so he declined to repeat his answer. I went through as many sports as I could think of, but for each suggestion I received a tight-mouthed defiance. I was now the enemy. I could now induce no more than a nod or shake of the head.

The others had disappeared by now and my attempts at patient pleasantness were becoming less convincing.

'Right, let's go back!' I said, standing up with an air of decisive insistence.

Negative response!

'If you won't go on, we've got to go back.'

Negative response!

'If you won't walk back, I'm going to have to carry you.'

I loomed over him, trying to suggest how physically superior I was.

Negative response!

'It's either walking back or me carrying you.'

Neither idea was acceptable. I sat back down defeated. Half an hour's virtual silence followed. I tried to appear nonchalant, though deep down I was sulking because of my ineffectiveness. Patrick at first was happy sucking grass and lying in the sun. Then he started looking in the direction the others had gone. He was obviously convinced they would return the same way they had come. I knew they were scheduled to return by a different route. I was going to tell him so, when our group appeared over a ridge and made their way towards us. Concern over Patrick had led to them changing their plans. Patrick led the way home with revitalised energy and enthusiasm.

Our worries about Patrick's eating habits were alleviated when Monsieur Girardot found a store of food in the wardrobe he was using. Thin, gaunt Patrick had been gorging himself on crisps, biscuits and cakes between meals. He had evidently seen no reason to disturb his normal diet. His secret supply having been discovered, he would bring a selection of his preferred delicacies to meal times. The sight of him eating about a dozen biscuits at breakfast was a little nauseating, but at least we knew he was starting the day on a full stomach.

It was Patrick's best friend, Philippe, who gave me the chance to observe a full range of French eating and drinking habits. He was particularly adept at drinking coffee, with a spoon trapped by his thumb, inside the bowl. He also practised the French habit of dunking bread into his coffee. He was not yet accomplished at the art, for the coffee would frequently drip onto his lap or the table. Others had mastered the skill of moving bread to mouth quickly, without wasting a drop. In addition he would mop up the remaining sauce from a meal with bread. Most French people do this solely to their plate, but Philippe was in the habit of mopping the table, not wishing to waste any of the juices splattered while the meal was being served.

Bread is an important part of the French diet. During most courses it is used as the second utensil, and as a result much is consumed. This is particularly so if the eater is a perfectionist, keen that there be not the slightest sign of the previous course on the plate. One course at the activity centre was a toasted ham sandwich, made with sliced bread. A basket of baguette chunks was placed on the table at the same time as the sandwich. It did seem like a touch of overkill. Apart from this one occasion the inclusion of fresh bread with a meal was a most acceptable habit. I was a little disappointed, though, that it was not automatically placed on the table with soup. This British practice has evidently not caught on in France.

Jean-Claude's problem occurred while rock-climbing and was a good example of the difficulty an instructor has in determining that thin line between disinclination and genuine fear. Jean-Claude had found moving up the rock face extremely hard. When he came to a section that jutted out, the thought of having to hoist his body over the protruding rock was too much for him. He froze. His feet, knees, body and hands clung tensely to the rock face. For him to move up or down became an impossibility. The instructor tried to calm, boost and entice him to make a move in an upward direction, but to no avail.

Eventually he virtually winched Jean-Claude to a position where he could continue the climb. After Jean-Claude had very tentatively abseiled down from the summit, the instructor engulfed him with back-slapping congratulations. But these were irrelevant. He knew he had failed. His pale face and tear-dampened eyes told the real story. He sat down, turning away from his friends to try and conjure a modicum of composure. His dark glasses became the answer. The normally lively Jean-Claude was totally subdued for the rest of the session. He declined the opportunity to climb the face a second time.

I don't think Jean-Claude will ever rock-climb again. His fear was such that he never gained the satisfaction others, who had found it difficult, felt, when reaching the top. The instructor had not judged the situation correctly, yet had he allowed everyone to come down immediately, a good half of the children would never have achieved their goal. And there is no doubt that those who reached the top felt an immense sense of achievement.

Mountaineering, along with archery and cycling, were the main sports during the week, though walking was the predominant activity. For four consecutive, half-day sessions, the children walked. Wednesday afternoon was spent trekking uphill to see some beavers. Once at the top, silence was asked for, as the animals were very shy. Then groups of ten were allowed to crouch on a cliff edge and, using binoculars, scout for the timid animals, who often sunbathed some three hundred metres away. The first two groups saw nothing, but when the last group was in position, one of the instructors spotted a beaver on a rock. Two or three of the children managed to see it before the call to return to base was given. When the other children had heard that one had been spotted I expected an outrage, because they were not to be allowed to return, to fulfil the purpose of the visit. Instead there were one or two disappointed faces; the rest readily accepted the situation. The children had been asked to remain virtually silent for an hour, so there needed to be a release of energy on the return trip. Rolling much of the way back was their response to the unrewarded discipline they had shown during the afternoon.

Thursday morning produced an almost identical set of circumstances. This time, though, a walk on the top of a volcano, to see a distant moufflon was the objective. The afternoon brought a walk in the forest with some interesting facts about trees and flowers, fungi and animal tracks. Amazingly the next morning had the same recipe: a walk in another part of the forest. The same instructor restated much of the same information. The children looked weary and vacant, only to be stirred by an unusual find, such as some fox droppings or a buzzard's feather.

I cannot help thinking that a group of British children would not be so compliant as their French counterparts. In France repetition is an accepted habit. To repeat what has already been said is commonplace, it being regularly used as a form of emphasis or simply a means of continuing a conversation. As a result children will not query continually going over old ground. It is part of their upbringing. British children, for the most part, do not possess such a high level of tolerance, and I feel sure would, in one way or another, be outwardly unhappy with a similarly unimaginative programme of activity.

In spite of my hypercritical comments, the week was a tremendous experience for these young children. They coped with being away from their parents extremely well and although the physical demands were immense, they enjoyed this chance to be self-sufficient.

Kate and Luke, of course, had their father watching their every other move, and through unwelcoming eye contact or a more insistent scowl, I was warned to keep my distance. I was slightly aggrieved at first that they didn't want a doting parent rushing to their assistance every time they had a problem. I quickly realized that their wish to be as independent as the others was a good sign. Not only did it show that they were no longer reliant on Polly and me, but that they felt comfortable in this totally French environment.

As we did not talk in French at home, I had rarely heard them speaking at great length. It was the speed at which they spoke that amazed me. They gave themselves no opportunity to think how to say something. Their replies were spontaneous and natural. We were only a week away from leaving France and they had become fluent in a second language.

17

EBB AND FLOW

I am a true towny. My knowledge of the country extends little further than that gained from an admiring glance from a car or train and afternoons out. Even those weekend trips into the countryside usually had an ulterior motive, like a bird garden or country house (with, of course, twentieth century amusements attached). To find a quiet spot in the British countryside, untainted by the cumbersome curiosity of the tourist, had not been considered. I had never stood to watch and appreciate the refinements of Nature. Such non-activity was a waste of time. There always had to be an end product in whatever I did. This year in Brittany gave me an opportunity to observe the natural world, not as a package tour excursion, but at a snail's pace.

The number and variety of butterflies to be found in our field in late summer was immense. To watch them innocently flickering from stem to bud, like an embarrassed eyelid, was both fascinating and soothing. The sweetcorn in the neighbouring fields was ripe for eating. Their plump cobs would bow with the breeze, as if in acquiescence, waiting for their coming decapitation.

During our evening meals we took to watching a particular spider who was patrolling one of the top frames of our French window. It would wait in one of the upper corners of the frame for a stray insect and then would shoot down, trying to wrap the surprised visitor in a strand of thread. If successful, it would swiftly encircle the victim with more of its web, until the innocent party was totally trussed. The now dead insect was hauled into the spider's own personal restaurant at the top of the window frame. To see it struggling to overcome a moth over twice its size was fascinating. Usually it failed, yet occasionally it succeeded, using its trusty thread to good effect.

Our armchair sport was one day suddenly terminated, when the French window was opened to allow in some fresh air. The spider decided to explore untrodden ground and was unceremoniously splattered between door and frame. We had shown no sympathy towards the moths and flies and likewise showed no remorse for the loss of the spider. Had a painted lady butterfly become entangled in its web, I am sure I would have jumped to its aid. Oh to be beautiful!

Crane flies were with us in abundance in October. We soon learned that to leave the windows open and the lights on in the evening attracted these oddities of Nature. Large and slow-moving, they were easy targets for a frustrated human. Even so it would take perhaps ten minutes to swat enough of the intruders to prevent further irritation that evening.

The most remarkable collection of crane fly occurred as a result of my leaving the shutters of one window unfastened and slightly ajar. A massive cluster had been attracted by the beckoning gap. I counted sixty-three begging to enter, give or take a long leg or two. The shutters remained unlocked that night.

Have you watched a leaf fall from bough to ground? I haven't. Each leaf I cast my gaze on refused me permission, as if to do so would release the secret of life. I could easily follow one a split second after it had left its branch on its haphazard journey to the ground. But to see a leaf in the moment of disengagement proved an impossibility. Like a watched kettle, the leaf will also not allow the human eye to notice any perceptible change of colour in autumn. The trees' flamboyant displays of yellows, oranges and reds are obviously brought about by the dryads on their unobserved, nightly jaunts.

Winter is the season of silence. The hibernating animal is not the only thing that sleeps; everything is inactive. Only the weather and food-seeking birds remind us that Nature is simply dormant. The venom of frost highlights Nature's reasons for inactivity. Frost will sit undaunted on the fields, which have been turned, flattened and turned again by the farmer, before being deserted until spring. It is there, displaying false purity, as an enticement for any living thing to break its surface and admire its beauty. Nature normally declines the offer. Only during a warm spell will plants and bushes inquisitively peep out through newly formed buds to see if it is spring. One rose became particularly curious and cheekily tried to blossom in February. It was ruthlessly dealt with before it could unfurl, and was left a pallid shadow of its normal splendour.

The sky on a frosty night is remarkably different in character from that in summer. The positioning of the stars is immaterial. The winter stars have an angry, piercing stare to them, whereas in summer they twinkle hazily. It seems that the gods have decided on the nature of each season and are imparting their wishes through the stars.

I developed an interest in the night sky while in France. In Britain my view of the sky had virtually always been cloistered by buildings. This lessened the panoramic impact that can be gained in the country, where the horizon can be seen in every direction.

The coast in winter time can also be compelling: the virgin sand with its drifts and curves, formed by wind and tide, the envy of any sculptor seeking perfection; the coastland trees, refusing to look the wind in the face; the tide, with its voice more enigmatic and eerie, without tourist distractions.

Springtime brought life back to the countryside: the trees' rehabilitation, the buds swelling and opening out, to find power from the sun to reach their zenith of attraction. In April the farmers' ploughs were to be seen everywhere as they churned the docile earth. Underneath was a rich, brown, fertile colour, full of strength for the growing season. Use of manure was eye-wateringly evident.

The crops flourished. Tiny shoots of corn, protected by long, weed-choking, plastic strips, tentatively poked through the ready-made holes. They grew in strength, until their undulating rows began to dominate their field, pleased with their balanced diet of rain and sun.

One of Nature's unexpected moments was a hailstorm in springtime. It certainly took the cows in the nearby field unawares. They seemed completely disorientated by this out-of-season phenomenon. They dashed around in an uncoordinated frenzy, swishing their tails frantically, to try to rid themselves of this unnatural barrage.

Two feral pigeons were undeterred by the fluctuations in the weather. They were preoccupied in nesting in a fir tree, close to our lounge window. We often watched the industrious male and female carrying twigs and grass to their nest. The female's role changed as she was obviously involved in laying and tending her eggs.

Soon two open-mouthed beaks were spotted, then a week later a light-grey head with just a single eye showing, peered at us through the shade of the surrounding leaves. They seemed to grow very quickly and it was not long before one of the young birds was standing on the edge of the nest, practising its flying skills. The next day I eagerly took up position with my camera, hoping to catch one or other of the fledglings' first uncontrolled flight from the tree. To my disappointment, Nature again concealed this special moment. Instead, watching them preen and vigorously flutter from branch to branch had to suffice.

A Siamese cat was similarly disappointed. It had somehow sensed the young birds' impending flight and was prowling more regularly than usual. To counteract such a foe, either the mother or father would float and flap its way round the tree, giving its young novices high-pitched vocal support.

Once they had learnt their magical art, like wayward adolescents, they rarely returned to their nest. They were occasionally seen in a tête-à-tête with their parents in the evening, though normally they were exploring other pastures, living life to the full.

The grass kept its greenness throughout June and into July. Grass cuttings maintained a fresh, vibrant smell for days. Global warming was not a burning issue during the early part of the summer. It was the worst June in three hundred years. Summer simply never came.

18

ABROAD THOUGHTS FROM HOME

Parting apéritifs and handshakes, gardening and cleaning, packing and discarding took up the vast majority of our last week in France. It was then that the grass started looking particularly long and the weeds became more apparent. The scratches on the wooden floors, the ink mark on the armchair and the effects of 'yellow tack' on the walls became very noticeable. The amount of necessities we had accumulated seemed considerable.

We knew that Brian, our co-transporter of belongings the previous September, had inconsiderately changed his car from an estate to a saloon and that our return could not be completed in the same way. As a result we had foisted a case or box on any visitors with the slightest chink of space in their car. Even though it would necessitate a 'round Britain tour' to retrieve our chattels, it was preferable to hiring a van. Jenny and Bob had thankfully arrived with a camper van, so they took most of the larger items. Despite this, it was plaintively obvious that we were to endure a claustrophobic return trip.

Surreptitious hiding of toys that Polly or I didn't like, at the bottom of a bag of rubbish, became common practice. Precious pictures were screwed tightly into a ball, revealing none of the features that could identify them, and were binned. Luckily one of my favourite sweaters, thin at the elbow and having lost its shape, was kept, to continue its life as a member of my wardrobe of working clothes. Our attempts to minimize the car load were slightly hindered by some of our new-found friends' generosity at our leaving. The most awkward of these gifts was the sack of about fifteen kilos of freshly dug, new potatoes.

Our last day started badly. Justin and John, the joint owners of our house (correction, the house) arrived an hour earlier than expected. Chairs were on tables, luggage was in disorganized piles, the oven was 'afoam', cleaning was in progress. Having seen the state of their heart's desire, they decided to erase this unconsidered image before them by going to the supermarket, in the hope that when they returned, their memory of their house would be reinstated.

As on the outward journey there was to be no vision through the back window. The back seat was also full with bags and boxes, there being just a moulded space for Kate and Luke. But there was still a cluster of essentials on the lounge carpet. I had a great idea.

'Why doesn't one of us sit in the back with one of the children on our lap? The rest of the luggage can be fitted in the front.'

'A great idea!' said Polly in a very complimentary tone. 'I'll drive.'

And so it was. There was, though, a reversal of roles when we reached England. Kate sat on my lap rather than Luke.

Justin and John returned to find their image of the house more or less restored, the house was checked, the finances were adjusted and readjusted. All that was left to do before our departure was to collect the children from their last morning in school.

The children had changed school twice before. Even so there had never been such an emotional final scene. The normally perfunctory kisses became meaningfully long, meant to implant a feeling of love for life. Kate struggled to the car with three friends clinging to her. Manuella, having said goodbye once, ran out of the playground for a final glimpse of her two friends. Her vigorous wave and broad smile could not disguise her tearful eyes.

Kate and Luke were both upset at leaving. They could both have happily continued to live in France. For the next few days Luke, when tired, shed a few tears at losing his friends. Kate, though, was more controlled. I asked her if she felt like crying on the last day of school. She said she did but fought back the tears by telling herself that she would be back to see her friends again.

Their last day at school had been sad, yet when they had distanced themselves from a year away, their reflections were more meaningful. They had missed the more creative approach which abounds in most British primary schools. In

France adherence to the strict boundaries of the National Curriculum has led to instruction being the most common teaching method. Learning facts about the local authority's administration network (could civic instruction have replaced religious education in the French curriculum?) was euphemistically uninspirational.

In the summer term, children from a number of primary schools in the area had been practising for a concert, *Au Choeur des Saisons*, to be held in the *Salles des Fêtes* in Lamballe. The parents dutifully assembled to watch their offspring. The first half of the programme consisted of a group of about fifty children (including Luke) chanting song after song non-stop for twenty-five minutes. The audience's glazed interest was revitalized by two of the choir pinching one another during the last two songs. There was no attempt to include any dramatic interpretation or children playing musical instruments; it was merely a matter of standing and reciting. The only sign of creativity was in the crêpe paper headdresses representing the four seasons, that each child wore. Sadly they made them look a trifle ridiculous.

The second half of the programme consisted of a group of about fifty children (including Kate) chanting song after song non-stop for twenty-five minutes. The songs were different but the headdresses were the same. Again there was some respite for the parents. After ten minutes some of the participants in the first half, finding the older children's rendering less than compelling, started to play a form of chase on their knees in front of the stage. (True creativity at last.) This was surprisingly not halted by parents or teachers, their full attention obviously attracted by the main event. The children soon found a way to get under the stage, where they continued their giggling game. Within a few minutes an irate woman, (it transpired that she was not one of the parents), back bent so as not to distract everyone else's concentration, rushed forward, grabbed the nearest available limb, a leg, and dragged it and the boy attached, from under the stage. This brought a halt to the alternative entertainment. Vigorous applause greeted the last song, though to me it was rather hollow-sounding, in the half-filled hall.

Little educational value seemed to have been gained from the evening's event. Although the children had worked as a team, gained experience in appearing before an audience and proved they could learn about twenty-five minutes worth of song, there was nothing of themselves in the performance. In all fairness, learning by rote plays a big part in exam success in French schools. Exams in France invariably centre around regurgitation of facts; therefore practice in learning information is very important.

I cannot help thinking that part of the reason for Kate and Luke's ability to cope with the French education system had much to do with the way they had been taught in Britain. They had been used to enquiring, making, experimenting, doing. As a result they had developed strategies to cope with many situations. They were well-practised in using their initiative, so when introduced to all the problems a French school posed they did not react like bemused fishes, but sought ways of doing the best they could in the circumstances.

I feel sure that if the roles were reversed, French children would have far greater difficulty in Britain. Having been brought up on a diet of spoon-fed information, they would find the more pupil-centred approaches in a British school as a much more unmanageable prospect.

As well as a rigid style of teaching, there is generally more stringent discipline in French schools. This is reinforced by the pressurising demands of the National Curriculum and more vociferous parental concern.

Despite this, school uniform, for the most part, is not felt essential to maintain disciplinary and educational standards. This is the case for staff as well as pupils. The chalk-flecked, off-the-peg sports jacket or tweed skirt, made to endure the most hazardous of classroom environments for decades, is felt to be immaterial. Teachers and pupils are dressed casually. Denim dungarees would not make an appearance at a British school's open evening, though Monsieur Girardot's did during Moncontour School's big day of the year.

To me, an image that goes alongside the word 'discipline' is a grey and depressing corridor. In France that image is not often far from the truth. Total dependence on the requirements of the National Curriculum appears to have allowed little time for interesting displays and attractive classrooms. This is surprising when looking at how important presentation is to the French shopkeeper.

This drab, almost insensitive approach to the learning environment can be seen at all levels of the education system. When Polly took her commercial exam in Paris, she was asked to go to the Maison des Examens. It is a massive grey building, which is as sombre inside as out. Candidates were to meet at eight o'clock for a half past eight start. This ensured that most people had an unsettling, early-morning dash through the rush-hour Paris. On arrival Polly found long queues outside each of the three ladies' toilets. The nervous needs of candidates had obviously not been considered in the planning of the building. The poor facilities were highlighted even more at lunchtime, for there was no canteen, not even a coffee machine.

The exam hall catered for about 200 students, necessitating the woman in charge to use a microphone to make herself heard. All the papers had not been given out by half past eight, but the exam machine was not allowed to be seen to falter. The exam started on time, regardless of the fact that some had to wait two or three minutes before they could begin.

The French education system seems to work more like a factory, with no elaborate trimmings. Every person is moulded for exams in the same way. (Even French children's handwriting shows little individuality.) They follow the same production line and are conditioned to produce model answers. If a pupil does not come up to standard, 'it' is sent back to the beginning for reprocessing, as was the case with Christine.

Could the French approach be a valid one? Such qualities as flair, individuality, common sense and adaptability may be innate and will be in evidence in adulthood, whether or not training and encouragement has been given. Therefore why not give children a basic factual knowledge, until they are of an age to cope with decision-making and the more perceptive aspects of education? In spite of the more dour, unimaginative approach to learning, the French are considerably more successful in persuading their young people to stay on in education than in Britain. Training, whether it be academic or vocational, is held in much higher esteem in France.

A lifetime in rural France was a very tempting idea, especially on a warm, wine-tinged evening. Certainly we had found no difficulty in being accepted by the people of Moncontour. Bretons are considered to be more aloof and less welcoming than most French people. There may well be some truth in this, yet if a foreigner is prepared to become involved in the community, that warmth and hospitality is readily in evidence. The sinister looks and dour, uninviting comments are more likely to be given to the house owner who is seen only a few times a year, when the sun is shining.

Before leaving Britain we had been aware that the grass is not always greener through rose-coloured glasses. As a result our original plans did not include becoming French residents. Therefore it was far more difficult to change direction, particularly as far as the children were concerned. Kate and Luke's approach to the experience was geared from the start towards returning to Britain at the end of the school year. For us then to decide we were remaining seemed to be almost unethical and could have led to feelings of resentment and mistrust.

I am sure some friends of friends would argue the opposite point of view. They had told their two teenage children that they were going on holiday to France. When they got there they told them they were staying for good. Had they explained their plans to their children from the start, an outward display of feelings could well have made them change their minds. In the event the children settled in French school extremely well, and none of the family have any regrets about the move.

Our promise that we would return to Britain was reinforced by a number of visits during the school holiday periods. There was a high level of concentration required by the children throughout the school day and time for unfettered relaxation was essential. France was unable to supply that necessary respite. Keeping direct contact with relatives and friends became very important and, despite the tiring journeys, it was an essential ingredient of the total experience.

We have grown to know and love Brittany and could pinpoint the places where we would gladly buy a second home. I am convinced that we could find as close to a bargain as possible in an ideal area. A good income could be gained from it, if only to cover the mortgage and running costs. As we would already be in France, the pressure to make a snap decision after a flying visit would not be there.

A couple who were obviously making a quick sally into Brittany to purchase a property, were lunching with an estate agent at a table near ours in a Dinan restaurant. They clung to the estate agent's every word. They were obviously putting their trust in him to lead them through the French house-buying minefield. He even made one or two suggestions as to what business would do well in Dinan.

'What this town needs is a top quality fish and chip shop?'

Food for thought?

We were in an ideal position so why have we decided not to buy? I am sure it would be possible to find someone reliable to maintain a property and supervise the comings and goings of holiday-makers. I am sure most of them would not abuse the property during their stay. Even so the house would start to belong to other people. Not being in complete control of a place that belongs to you is for some a strange sensation. It would almost be like the hideous feeling some people get when their home has been burgled. For ever after the place feels uncomfortable, tainted. To turn a cherished home into a business proposition was for us unthinkable.

Of course many people do not think this way and have been able to find that delicate balance between personal pleasure and personal gain. Of the people I have met who have bought in France, no one has talked of the speculation as a disaster. They have all maintained an unquenchable enthusiasm for owning property there. One couple who bought a virtual shell for very little are still enamoured with their acquisition. One speaks French and loves the country, the other's hobby is do-it-yourself. Money is tight, but at every opportunity they are in France, improving their property little by little.

Another couple have an attractive house which they let during the tourist season. Their income from letting it is less than they first thought, mainly because of maintenance requirements and a fairly short season. But there are no regrets. The house is to be their retirement home.

Another acquaintance has bought a fairly substantial property in France as a business speculation. He has underestimated the cost of using French builders and is disappointed to find how long it takes for the work to be done. Despite these difficulties I am sure his project will succeed. He has the necessary enthusiasm and ambition to ensure completion, together with that essential love of the French way of life. Business trips now take on a new dimension, for they involve being part of that unique atmosphere which is France.

France is tantalizing for so many British people. For most the ambiance gained from the annual holiday suffices. For others the need for contact with France is greater. For many the urge remains an unrequited frustration. There are just a few who have the courage and tenacity to cope with the complexities and upheaval caused by buying a French property. I am certain that having purchased, the strength of feeling for France will be the drive needed to make a success of the enterprise.

It is a shame that a touch of insanity (or being exceedingly rich) is needed to undertake that bold step across the Channel. The spirit of adventure seems to have been squashed in so many. It is as if leading politicians of the last fifty years, while advocating the importance of individuality, have secretly been concocting a strategy to enmesh the nation in a humdrum existence. To have vast numbers of the population satisfying inner desires and darting from one way of life to another might lead to economic instability. Therefore a structure, making people dependant on a regular income, had to be created. Hence the framework of our society has been so much built around the mortgage, consumerism and the retirement 'nest egg'. To break the mould would be fraught with danger.

As a result many people are denying themselves that basic, human need of a challenge. They have successfully built up a defence mechanism ('I can switch off') which has enabled them to cope with a stagnant working environment. With so many having reached their ultimate level of responsibility by the age of forty, it is difficult to envisage where they will find that vitality and drive needed to make the most of the last twenty-five years of their working lives.

We managed to extract ourselves from the edge of that unsatisfying malaise and have enjoyed every slow-moving, stressless minute of it. If I were ever worried about what to do in retirement, this year in France would have persuaded me to forget my concern. Having time on my hands has even brought satisfaction from doing the most menial of tasks. I found a perfectionist's pleasure in ensuring that the windows were clean, in defiance of the sun trying to uncover previously hidden smudges. There was time to prepare the cooking, rather than rely on thirty-minute, pre-packed, hunger fillers. There was time to consider the shape of the vine when trimming it, rather than snipping regardless, because you could only afford to allot half an hour for the task. In Britain I had begrudgingly played ball games with the children, soon finding an excuse to do something else. In France there was no rush, so these games became enjoyable and I tackled them whole-heartedly. Whether it was log-chopping or fire-lighting, squash or gymnastics, reading or writing, walking or driving, a full and active day always seemed to beckon.

POSTSCRIPT

We had been in England for a number of weeks before I phoned Mary to enquire after Sheena. It was a peculiar phone call. Every subject was covered other than dogs. If there was a pause in the conversation, one or other of us would quickly produce another topic of interest to discuss, keen to avoid broaching the inevitable. Eventually I asked how Sheena was.

'She's fine! Fully recovered from the operation. You couldn't believe she was eleven. She gets on really well with my sister's dog. . .'

Mary's exuberance said everything.

'We'd love to have her back, but if you really want to keep her, you can.'

'I'll keep her!' replied Mary, displaying admirable verbal reflexes.

We had prepared for losing Sheena by tempting Kate and Luke with two kittens, soon to be parted from their mother. The thought of the kittens certainly softened the blow, though Kate was still fairly upset.

Visits to Mary's house will be far more frequent than they used to be.